IN THE THEATER
OF CONSCIOUSNESS

IN THE THEATER
OF CONSCIOUSNESS

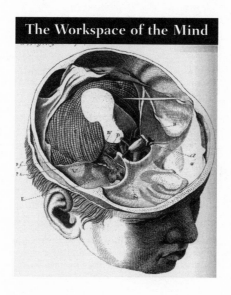

The Workspace of the Mind

BERNARD J. BAARS

New York Oxford • Oxford University Press • 1997

Oxford University Press

Oxford   New York
Athens   Auckland   Bangkok   Bogotá   Bombay   Buenos Aires
Calcutta   Cape Town   Dar es Salaam
Delhi   Florence   Hong Kong   Istanbul   Karachi
Kuala Lumpur   Madras   Madrid   Melbourne
Mexico City   Nairobi   Paris   Singapore
Taipei   Tokyo   Toronto

and associated companies in
Berlin   Ibadan

Library of Congress Cataloging–in–Publication Data
Baars, Bernard J.
In the theater of consciousness : the workspace of the mind /
Bernard J. Baars.
p. cm.   Includes bibliographical references and index.
ISBN 0-19-510265-7
1. Consciousness. 2. Intellect. 3. Human information processing.
4. Cognition. I. Title.
BF311.B227 1996
153—dc20 96-10379

1 3 5 7 9 8 6 4 2

Printed in the United States of America
on Acid-free paper

This book is dedicated to Francis H. C. Crick,
—who knows a fundamental scientific problem when he sees it—
for his leadership in bringing scientists back to consciousness

and

to those who advance freedom of speech and thought
wherever it may be under siege.

Preface

*E*ver since the *nova scientia* of Galileo and Copernicus began the revolutionary rise of modern physics, new sciences have been proclaimed with some regularity. Most of these announcements turn out to be false alarms. But today we actually find ourselves at one of those rare nodal points in the evolution of human understanding: For the first time in the hundred years since William James's *Principles of Psychology,* serious brain and psychological scientists are exploring conscious experience—often under obscure labels, but now with far better evidence and theory than ever before.

Only distant hints of the current ferment in scientific consciousness research have reached the public; some of the most fascinating findings and ideas have simply gone unnoticed. Yet our own consciousness is in many ways the most significant topic imaginable to us as human beings; nothing else is as close to us, and nothing has been as consistently baffling and mysterious to untold generations gone before. Urgent ethical questions depend on a better understanding of human consciousness, and in a world where science is often seen as a double-edged sword, the public has a natural interest in understanding developments at the frontier. As a cognitive neuroscientist with almost two decades of experience grappling with these questions, I thought it was high time to tell the story of some of the best scientific work available today. This book is the result.

The New Consciousness Science

The scientific race for consciousness is now on. Dozens of laboratories are focusing their efforts to be first with major new findings. Widely respected figures in neurobiology like Francis Crick, Gerald Edelman, Rodolfo Llinás, Michael Gazzaniga, and Joseph Bogen have already devoted many years to the enterprise. Psychologists Endel Tulving, Daniel Schacter, Hanna and Antonio Damasio, Morris Moscovitch, and others have studied memory after brain lesions with some remarkable results. Cognitive scientists who have made strong claims include Michael Posner, Tim Shallice, Daniel Schacter, and even myself. Philosophers are having a field day.

Human experience is a humbling problem, but one on which we can make step-by-step progress. Whole bodies of research in perception, selective attention, and immediate memory form a solid and reliable basis for this effort. In the last several years psychologists and brain imaging researchers have begun close and successful collaborations, so that we are beginning to see what the brain is actually doing when it is thinking and seeing and remembering, and much of the evidence fits our expectations. For the first time we can try to bring all these sources of information together to see if they make a unified story. Even as we do so, new findings appear each week. Today a sizable body of evidence points to the conclusion that consciousness is a key biological adaptation that makes it possible for the brain to interpret, learn about, interact with, and act upon the world.

This book is based on a framework for understanding the large domain of evidence bearing on our personal experience, called Global Workspace theory. GW theory presents a "theater model" in which consciousness requires a central workspace, much like the stage of a theater. It is set out in detail in my book *A Cognitive Theory of Consciousness* (1988) and in a series of technical publications.[1]

---

[1] Daniel C. Dennett and Marcel Kinsbourne (1992) have criticized a concept called a "Cartesian Theater, " which should probably be called the Cartesian Theater *Fallacy*. Three centuries ago René Descartes proposed that the conscious soul touches the physical body in a single point in the brain, the tiny pineal gland. Dennett and Kinsbourne maintain that the Cartesian Theater reflects a widely shared intuition that consciousness

Global Workspace theory is based on the belief that, like the cells of the human body, the detailed workings of the brain are widely distributed. There is no centralized command that tells neurons what to do. Just as each cell in the body is controlled by its own molecular code, the adaptive networks of the brain are controlled by their own aims and contexts. To organize this vast distributed domain there is a network of neural patches that work together to display conscious events. Today the best candidates for these loci of conscious experience may be the sensory projection areas of the cortex, where the great neural radiations coming from the eyes, the ears, and the body first reach the surface of the brain. A few small structures of the core brain stem and midbrain are essential to consciousness, but great quantities of tissue elsewhere in the brain can be lost without causing a loss of conscious experience. Conscious contents appear to be disseminated globally to a great multitude of networks throughout the brain that are unconscious, but that have observable conscious consequences downstream.

As it happens, all unified theories of cognition today are theater models. Global Workspace theory derives from the integrative modeling tradition of Allan Newell, Herbert A. Simon, John R. Anderson, and others in cognitive science. It is consistent with models of working memory by Alan Baddeley, the mind's eye by Stephen Kosslyn, explicit knowledge after brain damage by Daniel Schacter and others, the thalamocortical searchlight elaborated by Francis Crick, and society models outlined by Michael Gazzaniga and Marvin Minsky. The brain implications of Global Workspace theory have been explored by James Newman and myself. British mathematician John G. Taylor and others are working to apply modern "neural net" models to the problem. The convergence of ideas today is simply astonishing.

I have sprinkled this book with demonstrations that I hope will appeal to your personal experience, but that also yield reliable public reports of

involves such a single-point center. The Cartesian Theater is a fallacy, a *reductio ad absurdum*, not the sort of thing anyone today would seriously suggest. There is of course no single point in the brain where "everything comes together." We do know of numerous well-established brain maps of the world and of the body, and of convergence zones that integrate many different sources of information into some coherent account of current reality. There is solid evidence that some of these brain maps are conscious, and that others help shape conscious experience. But no scientific model today commits the Cartesian fallacy. Certainly none of the scientific theater models that have been proposed since the 1950s suggest that all conscious experiences come together in a single point. Real theaters are not constructed that way; they work just fine, and provide productive metaphors for thinking about the brain.

the kind we use in science. From a scientific point of view we cannot share your personal experience; we can deal only with your *descriptions* of your experiences. However, for many well-studied phenomena, the subjective observations and the objective evidence converge so well that the distinction has little practical significance. You could, if you wish, understand all the demonstrations in this book from a subjective point of view. Or conversely, you could pretend that none of the demonstrations apply to your own experience, and that we are exploring the objective behavioral and brain processes of an utterly unknown species infesting the surface of the third planet of Sol. Neither pretense is necessary, because the inside and outside points of view on the evidence tend to dovetail so well. The many convergent pieces of evidence persuade me at least that in practice, the famous gap between mind and body is a bit of a myth.

The really daring idea in contemporary science is that human conscious experience can be understood *without* miracles, just as it was Darwin's radical idea that the origin of species could be understood without divine intervention. We are beginning to see consciousness as a key biological adaptation with multiple functions. Conscious contents trigger a host of unconscious processes and are shaped in turn by unconscious *contexts*. Consciousness appears to be essential in integrating perception, thought, and action, in adapting to novel circumstances, and in providing information to a self-system. By comparison, the vast audience of *un*conscious knowledge sources seems to be much more isolated and autonomous.

Readers with access to the World Wide Web can use the names of researchers cited throughout this book, to find original books and articles.[2] Those interested in the history of behaviorism, introspectionism, and the emergence of cognitive psychology may wish to peruse my earlier book *The Cognitive Revolution in Psychology* (1986).

---

[2] A website with the author's work can be found at baars/wrightinst.edu. There are now several other useful sources, including three journals. *Consciousness and Cognition: An International Journal* contains original scientific contributions, and can be found at http://psych.pomona.edu /Cac/ CaC.html. *PSYCHE: A Journal of Consciousness Studies* includes scientific and philosophical articles at http://psyche.cs.monash.edu.au/. The *Journal of Consciousness Studies* is philosophical and somewhat more popular, see http://www.zynet.co.uk/ imprint. The last address also contains a set of abstracts on the emerging field of consciousness science. The Association of the Scientific Study of Consciousness encourages high-quality scientific and scholarly research, and can be reached at http://www.phil.vt.edu/ASSC/.

I owe an immense debt to scientists and philosophers whose dedicated work has helped us return to consciousness. In psychology and cognitive science, they include Michael Posner, Don Dulany, Ernest R. Hilgard, George A. Miller, Herbert Simon, Allan Newell, Endel Tulving, George Lakoff, Steve Palmer, Daniel Schacter, John Kihlstrom, Arthur Reber, Bruce Mangan, Tom Natsoulas, Ellen Langer, Donald Norman, George Mandler, John G. Taylor, Peter H. Greene, Donald G. MacKay, William P. Banks, Donald Broadbent, Alan Baddeley, Roger Shepard, Daniel Wegner, John Bargh, Geoffrey Underwood, Stephen LaBerge, David LaBerge, Antti Revonsuo, Terry Sejnowski, and many others. In philosophy, the indispensables include Daniel C. Dennett, John R. Searle, Owen Flanagan, Ned Block, David Chalmers, and Patricia and Paul Churchland. In neurobiology, I have learned much from the work of Francis Crick, Roger Sperry, Gerald Edelman, Joseph Bogen, Michael Gazzaniga, Steve Hillyard, Ron Mangun, Semir Zeki, Hannah and Antonio Damasio, V. S. Ramachandran, Morris Moscovitch, Allan Hobson, Nikos Logothetis, Risto Näatanen, James Newman, Oliver Sacks, David Galin, and Charles Yingling. In clinical psychology and psychiatry, I want to gratefully acknowledge Mardi J. Horowitz, Jerome S. Singer, David Spiegel, Joseph Weiss, and Lester Luborsky. Many others have my sincere gratitude.

Special thanks are owed for friendship and intellectual stimulation to William P. Banks, fellow editor and founder of *Consciousness and Cognition: An International Journal,* published by Academic Press, which has been a joy and an intellectual lifeline for five years; Bruce Mangan for his valuable insights into "fringe" consciousness; David Galin, Joseph Bogen, Jim Newman, and Michael Wapner for their rigorous thinking and friendship; Francis Crick, Christof Koch, and Stanley Klein for setting me straight on various aspects of neurobiology; Arthur Blumenthal for help in understanding the history of experimental psychology; Scott Slotnick for his competence, intelligence, and enthusiasm, and for reminding me what a remarkable privilege it is to be alive and working on these historic issues. Katie McGovern has given much intellectual feedback as well as the gift of her love and friendship; Megan and Chris McGovern helped keep me down to earth; Andrew McGovern helped correct the manuscript; and my parents, Louis and Lynn Baars, made it all possible. I am forever in their debt.

Berkeley, Calif.   B. J. B.
February 1996

Contents

Prologue: The Metaphor   3

« I » CARVING NATURE AT THE JOINTS

1. Treating Consciousness as a Variable   11

« II » A UNIFIED IMAGE

2. The Theater Stage Has *Limited Capacity* but Creates
   Vast Access   39

3. Onstage: Sensations, Images, and Ideas   62

4. The Spotlight: Attention, Absorption, and the Construction
   of Reality   95

« III » USING THE THEATER

5. Behind the Scenes: The Contexts that Shape Our Experience   115

6. Volition: Conscious Control of Action   130

7. The Director: Self as the Unifying Context of Consciousness   142

Contents

« IV » CONCLUDING THOUGHTS

8. What Is It Good For? The Functions of Consciousness   157

9. Epilogue: A Tiny Bit of Philosophy   165

    Appendix: Make your Own Theory: A Summary of the Evidence   169

    Selected References   183

    Index   189

IN THE THEATER
OF CONSCIOUSNESS

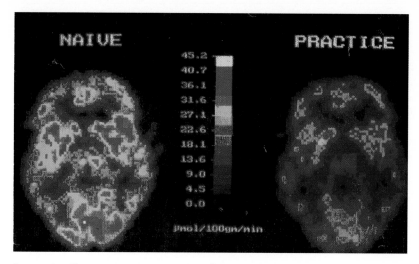

Insert 1. *Comparing conscious and unconscious events.*

Consider these two brain scans, showing the same person playing the computer game Tetris twice, four weeks apart. In the left scan, the computer game is just being learned. On the right, the bright colors have become duller, indicating a significant drop in brain activity. Is it because playing Tetris has become habitual and nearly unconscious after four weeks? It seems one reasonable interpretation. (Haier et al., 1992)

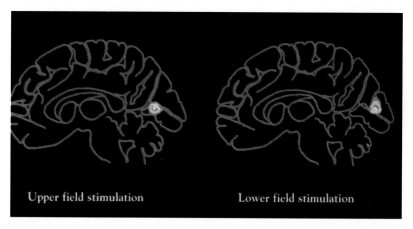

Upper field stimulation   Lower field stimulation

Insert 2. *Spectacularly accurate brain activation for a simple visual event.*

On the left side, the brain's owner is looking at a bright white screen above the point where the eyes are fixed; on the right, the bright screen is beneath the fixation point. The "hot spots" in the brain appear exactly where they should, in the earliest part of the visual cortex. When this area is damaged, *conscious* vision is lost, but the brain still analyzes input from the eyes *unconsciously.* This early area, called V1, seems to be needed specifically for *conscious* vision.

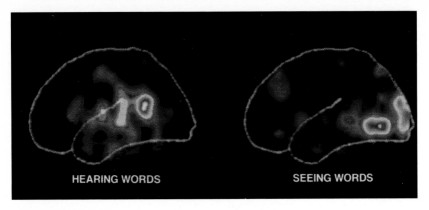

HEARING WORDS   SEEING WORDS

Insert 3. *Conscious activity in the sensory brain?*
   The left brain scan shows auditory cortex "lighting up" when a subject *hears* a set of words, but on the right side it is the visual cortex that activates when the subject *reads* the words. High brain activity does not always correspond to conscious experience. But when someone reports a specific conscious sensation at the exact moment when the area that represents the sensation becomes active, it begins to seem likely that we are actually seeing some of the brain structures for conscious sensation. (Posner and Raichle, 1994)

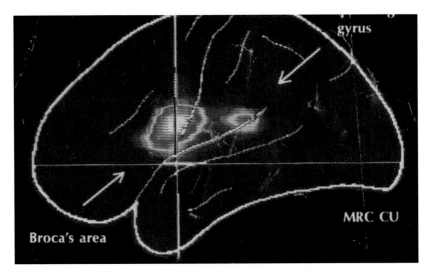

gyrus

MRC CU

Broca's area

Insert 4. *Quiet inner speech.*
   Most people walk around the world silently talking to themselves. This brain scan shows a subject doing just that. The large bright spot on the left shows high activity in the classical control center for vocal movement, while the smaller spot on the right is known to analyze speech sounds. Psychologists have long explored the inner speech component of "working memory"; today we can see it in the living brain. (Paulescu et al., 1993)

PROLOGUE:
THE METAPHOR

You are conscious and so am I. This much we can tell pretty easily, since when we are not conscious our bodies wilt, our eyes roll up in their orbits, our brain waves become large, slow, and regular, and we cannot read a sentence like this one.

While the outer signs of consciousness are pretty clear, it is our inner life that counts for most of us. The contents of consciousness include the immediate perceptual world; inner speech and visual imagery; the fleeting present and its fading traces in immediate memory; bodily feelings like pleasure, pain, and excitement; surges of feeling; autobiographical memories as they are recalled; clear and immediate intentions, expectations, and actions; explicit beliefs about oneself and the world; and concepts that are abstract but focal. In spite of decades of behavioristic denial, few would quarrel with this list today.

At this instant you and I are conscious of some aspects of the act of reading—the shape of *these letters* against the white texture of the page, and the inner sound of *these words*. But we are probably not aware of the touch of the chair, of a certain background taste, the subtle balancing of our body against gravity, a flow of conversation in the background, or the delicately guided eye fixations needed to see *this phrase*; nor are we now aware of the fleeting present of only a few seconds ago, of our affection for a friend, and of some of our major life goals. These unconscious elements are as important as the conscious ones because they give us natural comparison conditions.

For example: While you are conscious of words in your visual *focus*, you surely did not consciously label the word "focus" just now as a noun; yet this sentence would be incomprehensible if highly specialized language analyzers—located in the cortex of the brain, just above the left ear—did not label "focus" as a noun *unconsciously*. The meaning would change significantly if you understood it to be a verb or an adjective.

On reading "f-o-c-u-s," you were surely unaware of its nine alternative meanings, though in a different sentence you would instantly bring a different meaning to mind. What happened to the others? A wealth of evidence supports the notion that some of those meanings existed unconsciously for a few tenths of a second before your brain decided on the right one. Most words have multiple meanings, but only one can become conscious at a time. This seems to be a fundamental fact about consciousness.

These examples illustrate the sense of the word "consciousness" we wish to understand—that is, *focal* consciousness of easily described events, like "I see a printed page" or "He imagined his mother's face." A great body of evidence shows that such conscious contents can be reported *as conscious* with great accuracy under the right conditions. These conditions include immediate report, freedom from distraction, and some way for the outside observer to verify the report. These are standard laboratory conditions in thousands of experiments on sensory perception, memory, attention, and mental imagery. They also fit the demonstrations presented throughout this book.

Whenever a question about the meaning of consciousness arises in these pages, I invite you to revisit the paragraphs above. The meaning of "consciousness" intended here is best illustrated by your own experience. *Verifiable public report* is the key to scientific evidence, but *your experience here and now* is quite a good index to the evidence. All the subjective demonstrations used in this book can be tested objectively, and all the objective facts can be experienced by you and me. That is why we believe we can talk about consciousness *as such*.

The Metaphor

In Book 7 of Plato's *Republic* we find the following allegory:

> Imagine mankind as dwelling in an underground cave. . . in this they
> have been since childhood, with necks and legs fettered, so they have to
> stay where they are. They cannot move their heads round because of the
> fetters, and they can only look forward, but light comes to them from fire
> burning behind them. . . . Between the fire and the prisoners. . . imagine a
> low wall has been built, as puppet showmen have screens. . . then bearers
> carrying along this wall all sorts of articles which they hold. . . statues
> of men and other living things, made of stone or wood. . . . What do you
> think such people would have seen of themselves and each other
> except their shadows, which the fire cast on the opposite side of the
> cave?. . . such persons would certainly believe that there were no realities
> except those of those shadows. . . . [Plato, p. 312]

Plato's famous Allegory of the Cave has odd and unexpected resonances down the ages in Western thought, and in Asian philosophy as
well. Indeed, two and a half millennia later another observer wrote,

> A common metaphor is that of a "spotlight" of visual attention. Inside
> the spotlight the information is processed in some special way. This
> makes us see the attended object or event more accurately and more
> quickly and also makes it easier to remember. Outside the "spotlight" the
> visual information is processed less, or differently, or not at all. The
> attentional system of the brain moves this hypothetical spotlight rapidly
> from one place in the visual field to another, just as, on a slower time
> scale, you move your eyes. [Crick, 1993, p. 62]

Plato's point was the fallibility of conscious perception compared to
the eternal verities of philosophy, while Francis Crick was aiming to
understand the relationship between the brain structure called the
thalamus and the great cerebral cortex, both necessary for conscious
experience. What is the difference between Plato's fire-cast shadows
and Crick's thalamic spotlight? I feel moved as much by the similarities as the differences: both are unifying conceptions of human consciousness. In fact, both seem to reflect the same underlying metaphor
of our personal experience, the *theater metaphor*.[1] Plato's Allegory of

---

1. Readers wishing to compare cognitive theater models to the "Cartesian Theater" of
Daniel C. Dennett and Marcel Kinsbourne, should see the footnote on page viii–ix.

the Cave may be more elaborate, but Crick's spotlight has a more solid basis in brain anatomy and physiology. A number of cognitive and brain scientists have suggested versions of the theater metaphor, and in ancient times the same theme was sounded in Vedanta philosophy; at various moments in Western thought, and surely by poets and philosophers in many other times and places.

Theater models have become attractive again today, as scientists have realized how much of the brain's work is done unconsciously, by innumerable small bits of specialized brain tissue. This may be hard to realize from our own experience, but just look at the brain:

1. The brain has on the order of one hundred billion nerve cells.
2. Each nerve cell has about ten thousand inputs (dendrites) from other neurons, and only a few outputs (axon terminals).
3. Neurons are so interconnected that one can get from one cell to any other cell in the brain in seven steps or less.
4. Most of the brain consists of small assemblies of brain cells, arrays, columns, maps, clusters, networks, functional routines, and great swaths of cable connections, all with highly specific functions. Some nerve cells pick up point sources of red light in a single location in the visual field. Others specialize in short lines oriented forty-five degrees above the horizontal. Still others recognize faces or coordinate sights with sounds. Specialization is the name of the game for most neurons. But the great bulk of these tissues are unconscious.

The brain seems to show a *distributed style of functioning,* in which the real work is done by millions of specialized, sophisticated systems without detailed instructions from some command center. By analogy, the human body also works cell by cell; unlike an automobile, it has no central engine that does all the work. Each cell is specialized for a particular function according to instructions encoded in its DNA, its history, and chemical influences from other tissues. And the cell is of course the body's basic unit of organization. In its own way the human brain shows the same distributed style of organization.

The theater metaphor is useful because a great array of evidence indicates that *consciousness creates access* to many knowledge sources in the brain. And yet only a fraction of the brain seems to directly support conscious experience. This consciousness network seems to include the sensory areas of the cortex, perhaps some surrounding areas, and a few subcortical structures; together they provide the stage for the unconscious audience in the rest of the brain. Consciousness seems to be the publicity organ of the brain. It is a facility for *accessing, disseminating, and exchanging information*, and for *exercising global coordination and control.*

As it happens, all of our unified models of mental functioning today are theater metaphors; it is essentially all we have.[2] They are called by a variety of names and have been developed over the last forty years based on a vast range of evidence, from studies of chess players to work on inner rehearsal, from mental rotation of visual images to the subtle effects of brain damage. A remarkable group of distinguished scientists have devoted careers to these integrative conceptions of human cognition.

What has not been done so far is to forge a working link between these great bodies of thought and the core issue of human experience.

That is the aim of this book.

2. Neural net models, developed over the last ten years, have led to important theoretical insights. Neural nets do a superior job of modeling some phenomena of consciousnesss, but they do not easily reflect its large-scale architectural properties. One promising approach is to build hybrid architectures combining neural nets with theater models.

Part I

CARVING NATURE
AT THE JOINTS

*W*hat evidence is relevant to consciousness as such? This has been one of the most difficult questions for psychologists and brain scientists to contend with. It has led to great philosophical controversy; but a scientific consensus is now emerging, so that in research circles the debate has faded.

As everywhere else, evidence for consciousness is that which "carves nature at the joints." In this case, it involves experimental comparisons between very similar conscious and unconscious mental processes, that is, comparisons that allow us to treat consciousness as a variable. The closer the comparison, the more it tells us about the differential effects of consciousness. Waking up this morning compared to being in deep sleep a few minutes before, provides one example. Or compare the things you are paying attention to at this moment to the information you are ignoring: the touch of your chair, your unexpressed thoughts and feelings, that sound in the background. A third comparison is your memory of this morning's breakfast, before and after conscious recall. There are dozens of such comparisons, and together they place strong empirical bounds on our conception of conscious experience.

one

TREATING CONSCIOUSNESS
AS A VARIABLE

> There is no more important quest in the whole of science probably than the attempt to understand those very particular events in evolution by which brains worked out that special trick that enabled them to add to the cosmic scheme of things: colour, sound, pain, pleasure, and all the other facets of mental experience.
> —ROGER SPERRY

We can only study something if we can treat it as a variable, comparing its presence to its absence. A number of historic breakthroughs in science emerged from the realization that some previously assumed constant, like atmospheric pressure or gravity, was actually a variable. It required a great leap of imagination for natural philosophers to understand that all objects in the universe need not fall toward the earth, that gravity could be *different* elsewhere in the universe. Newton's ability to make that leap led to the solution of the ancient puzzle of planetary motion.

Consciousness has seemed to be different from all other scientific concepts; it has been extraordinarily difficult to treat it as a variable. The persistent pattern over centuries has been to see our own experience as the only psychological domain that can be conceived, one that has no kinship to any conceivable comparison condition. Our own consciousness is hard to study because we cannot vary it; as soon as we lose consciousness, we can no longer observe anything. And how can we observe someone else's conscious experience?

It is actually quite possible to compare conscious events that people can report accurately to unconscious ones that can be inferred and studied indirectly. Scientists have now explored a number of cases in which we believe conscious and unconscious conditions to be quite comparable. We know a great deal about normal versus subliminal perception; attended versus nonattended speech; novel versus routine and automatic processes; explicit compared to implicit memory; and much more.

We can call this method *contrastive phenomenology,* to emphasize the involvement of private experience. Phenomenology is the study of consciousness based on subjective reports; in scientific practice we always supplement subjective reports with objectively verifiable methods. Our basic evidence about sensory perception, dreaming, memory, and thinking is all of this kind. Thus in modern science we practice a kind of verifiable phenomenology.

The fact that we study private experiences in science is often disguised by our language and methodology. We prefer to talk about public reports of conscious experiences. But there is generally such a close mapping between objective reports and subjective experiences that in this book for all intents and purposes we can talk of *your phenomenology,* your consciousness as you experience it. You can demonstrate all the basic properties that have begun to emerge to yourself.

Mozart was a master of consciousness. Only a composer of the highest musical order could open the delectable *Sinfonia Concertante* on a *single note,* played by the solo violin and viola in perfect unison an octave apart, two indistinguishable sounds except for the unearthly depth of the added harmonics. *One note*—think about it. Only a master could bounce madly from Leporello's low buffoonery in the first scene of *Don Giovanni* to the Don's botched attempt to seduce Don'Anna, a fight to the death, more clowning, and finally Don'Anna's furious cry of *vendetta!*—changing mood in seconds while maintaining a seamless flow of light and tender commentary in the orchestra—and somehow combine all these extreme and incompatible elements into a sparkling conscious unity.

While writing this chapter in Denmark, I had a chance to visit the great domed cathedral in the old capital city of Roskilde, where seven centuries of Danish royalty lie buried. Standing in the ancient church it became suddenly clear that it is not a *building* in the modern sense at all. The Domkirke is a many-layered storytelling domain. Every niche is filled with symbols, gravestones, allegories, reminders, and warnings about the pride and power of kings and queens, and the evocative stories of the faith. No one could take it all in at once; one would have to go back many times, exploring its meanings layer by layer, as did the people who worshiped in it for generations. The cathedral was a massive effort to shape the beliefs and fantasies of its people, even as a television program shapes the beliefs and fantasies of children today. But the cathedral was not only for children; it had deeper meaning, more profound attachment to life's joys and terrors, more reminders of the certainty of death, more promises of life after death if one obeyed, more propaganda (in the original meaning of the word) designed to propagate the faith.

In a way scientific exploration of human consciousness is just an extension of the arts, theater, literature, and even religion. We are returning to a project that has moved human beings for centuries: to apply the mind to its own understanding. I can imagine nothing more thrilling and ultimately practical.

The Challenge

For years it was common to hear scientists say that human consciousness was unlike any other scientific problem, in that it was not at all clear what evidence was relevant to it; as for theory, it seemed so far beyond our comprehension that it was hardly worth talking about. The trouble is that predictions of failure are self-fulfilling. If we are convinced that we cannot ever learn about our own experience, we will not even try to understand it, and then we will indeed remain as uninformed as ever. Such all-devouring skepticism seems unreasonable.

Consciousness may not be a solvable problem. In physics the exact gravitational dance of three bodies in space is believed to be unsolvable. In biology, recapturing the precise genetic pressures that led to a given mutation millions of years ago is not possible. There are other questions that are simply not possible to answer, perhaps ever. Nature does not come with guarantees. The question remains, is consciousness something that can be known?

Consciousness: A Big Phenomenon

A useful rule of thumb in science is to go for the big phenomena first, those that stand out like great craggy mountains from the plain—things like gravity, color, and the astonishing family resemblances between animals dwelling continents apart. Once we see them, the big phenomena seem so obvious that you have to *try* to overlook them. That is where the early payoffs can be found for research; subtleties come later.

Consciousness often seems to be the biggest, loudest phenomenon we could possibly study. No alien space visitor could fail to observe that vertebrates, including humans, engage in purposeful motion only two-thirds of the earthly day. In the remaining third, we hibernate. Coming back to consciousness in the morning, we humans report a rich and varied array of experiences: colors and sounds, feelings and smells, images and dreams, the rich pageant of everyday reality. We rise and begin to engage in purposeful action. Our brains begin a whole new mode of functioning. In this broad sense, the centrality of consciousness is pretty much beyond doubt.

It is sometimes said that there is no known brain index of consciousness, but that is not true. Place two electrodes on any spot on a person's scalp (silver dimes will do), connect wires to the coins, and hook the wires in turn to your stereo amplifier. Show the stereo output on a video screen, and you will see large, slow, regular electrical waves while your subject is in deep sleep, followed by small, rapid, irregular wavelets when he or she wakes up. Even such gross electrical signals, seeping through layers of skin and bone, show the conscious state to be utterly different from deep sleep or coma. It is not a subtle sort of thing.

Now imagine science as a great community effort to fit together an enormous cut-out puzzle, too large for any single mind to solve, with big and small pieces. Which do you start with? The advantage of starting with the big pieces is that they constrain many others; the smaller ones don't tell us nearly as much. It is for that reason, if for no other, that conscious experience is such a vital scientific issue. It is a great central piece that locks many others into place.

Teasing Out the Essentials

We live in the middle of a gravity well, a local maximum of gravitational attraction that makes it expensive in energy to escape into space. But the effects of the earth's gravity on our bodies has become so predictable to each of us that its very existence goes unnoticed. The discovery of variable gravity was the intellectual breakthrough needed to understand bodies in motion, one that solved many problems as soon as it clicked into place. Overcoming our earthbound perspective was an essential precondition for classical physics.

A hundred years ago naturalists had to *learn* to think of species as variable. Animal and plant species are stable over the human life span, and our intuitive notion of immutable species is by no means irrational or dumb. If few naturalists before Charles Darwin believed in evolution, it was in part because of the unbelievable amount of time needed for species to evolve, and in part because evolution broke the boundaries of the comforting human-sized universe as told in Genesis. Whatever the reason, seeing species as variable over time made it possible to understand how saber-tooth tigers could be close relatives of house cats, and how farmyard chickens could be evolutionary cousins to *Tyrannosaurus rex*. Seeing an assumed constant as a variable was the key.

The same perspective trick has worked at other turning points in history. Relativity theory turned space-time into a variable. Plate tectonics changed the continents into floating slabs of earth crust, and Riemannian geometry bent Euclid's parallel lines into converging arcs. Again and again we have been obliged to go beyond our local world with its predictable gravity, immutable plants and animals, flat and immovable surfaces, stable atmospheric pressure, and well-defined accepted beliefs. As life's constants become relativized, all the certainties we live by become frighteningly unpredictable for a while. The pay-off, of course, is insight.

Consciousness has seemed to be different from all these scientific concepts; it has been almost impossible to treat as a variable. The persistent pattern over written history has been to see conscious experience as the *only* psychological domain that can be conceived, one that has no kinship to any conceivable comparison condition.

In the year 1637, Descartes expressed the view that everything in the mind must be conscious. He wrote:

> [T]here can be nothing in the mind. . .of which it is not aware, this seems to me self-evident. For there is nothing that we can understand to be in the mind. . .that is not a thought or dependent on a thought. (p. 171)

In the early Enlightenment this suggests an image of the mind as a sunny little room, in which one can look around and see the daylight shining through the window, the bright flowers on the table, the portrait on the wall. We can be conscious of everything in this little room, even ourselves. There is no unconscious in this sunlit early Enlightenment mind, just a turning of attention from one thing to another. Of course if there is no unconscious knowledge, because consciousness has no comparison condition.

By wide consent the foremost work on human mental processes, even today, is William James's *Principles of Psychology*, which appeared in 1890. The *Principles* offers thirteen hundred pages of inspired dialogue on the major topics of psychology. Building on fifty years of European studies, it has given us classic descriptions of selective attention, mental imagery, hypnosis, habit and effortful concentration, the stream of consciousness, the basic arguments for and against unconscious processes, a theory of voluntary control and impulsiveness, the crucial distinction between self-as-subject and self-as-object, and much more. On many of these topics James's thinking is fully up to date, and it is embarrassing but true that much of the time he is still ahead of the scientific curve.

Entire research domains have been inspired by single passages in the *Principles*. Attention researchers routinely cite James's passage on selective attention as the definition of their topic (see Chapter 4). Other seminal passages describe the limits of immediate memory, the "tip-of-the-tongue" phenomenon, the use of conscious images to control voluntary action, and the central role of habit and automaticity.

And yet *The Principles of Psychology* contains a crucial flaw. Along with sparkling insights, stated with unequaled clarity and verve, James was convinced the mind was limited to conscious processes alone. James believed that consciousness was the sole instance of mentality, while *un*conscious events were "only physical." The two were different metaphysical substances. It was impossible to treat consciousness as a variable, and as a result it was impossible to study its effects.

Most people in the nineteenth century agreed with James: "unconscious intelligence" was a bizarre oxymoron to our great-grandparents. Consciousness was the crown of human reason; unconsciousness was merely a bodily function. Only toward the end of the nineteenth century did scientific thinkers—notably Pierre Janet in Paris and Sigmund Freud in Vienna—begin to infer unconscious processes quite freely, based on posthypnotic suggestion, jokes, neuroses, slips of the tongue, and the like. Freud's ideas have achieved so much influence among the educated public that the art and literature of our time is incomprehensible without them. But Freud had curiously little impact in scientific psychology and brain science because his claims about unconscious influences could not be tested in a persuasive way.

Behavioristic scientists after James's death in 1910 rejected the whole business of conscious experience because it seemed rife with endless, useless perplexities. Naturally they made little progress on understanding consciousness during their seven decades of dominance because they had no way of thinking about *either* conscious or unconscious processes. They, too, were unable to view consciousness as a variable. Neither William James nor B. F. Skinner could apply the experimental method to the most humanly important topic of all.

The Cognitive Unconscious

There is now solid evidence that for most conscious events we can find unconscious ones of comparable complexity. Unconscious routines are believed to be involved in all mental tasks, though they seem to lack the unity, coherence, and accessibility of conscious experiences.

The simplest pattern of findings comes from subliminal presentation of words. After years of controversy psychologists Norman Dixon and Anthony Marcel finally provided persuasive results that words presented too fast to identify consciously are still processed in the brain, at least to the level of meaning. A subliminal word like /dog/ makes it easier to identify /puppy/ as a real word a few seconds later. Hundreds of careful subliminal studies have been published over the last ten years, and this unconscious "priming effect" now looks very reliable.

Subliminal processes seem quite limited, however. Anthony Greenwald has recently shown that two-word compounds such as *honey cake,* *rat hole,* and *potato soup* cannot be combined into single unified concepts subliminally. Instead, they are treated as single words—*honey, cake, rat,* and *hole.* Combining two words into a single concept seems to require consciousness. And there is little evidence that subliminal stimuli can influence our actions or attitudes. One cannot flash BUY COKE on a movie screen and expect to increase Coca-Cola sales during intermission. But unconscious word identification does exist.

Even more persuasive has been research on automaticity of highly practiced skills, especially automatic language processing. When you and I read a sentence such as this one, we do much more work unconsciously than consciously. Learning a language is largely a process of establishing automatic routines for word recognition, syntactic inference, and semantic interpretation. All those hours young children spend listening to older people talking, with little or no understanding, do pay off in the most intellectually remarkable feat of our lives, the conquest of language. Becoming a skilled speaker means paying attention (*being conscious* of sounds and meanings), but over time each new discovery becomes automatic and unconscious, as it must, because the vast complexity of language analysis would otherwise overwhelm our limited conscious capacity.

All that has become clear only recently. Over the centuries our own experience has been so compelling that most people have been simply unable to believe that unconscious processes could be anything like conscious ones. Consciousness was literally incomparable.

If we live at a historic time today for the study of human experience, it is not just because we have more facts, but because we can treat consciousness as a variable like so many others. The evidence discussed in this book comes from a large set of comparisons between conscious and unconscious processes.

Today, remarkable new brain imaging techniques are showing us the heartbeat of the living brain. Psychological methods have been honed to a sharp edge, so that we now routinely measure the time course of mental processes down to a few tens of milliseconds. We have much better ways of modeling mental processes than ever before. But the best technical tools are of no help if we cannot *think* with clarity. That is one of our aims.

Contrastive Phenomenology: The Experimental Method

Insert 1 in the color section presents a visual image you may want to keep in mind to symbolize experimental comparisons in which we try to keep everything constant except the degree of consciousness of whatever is going on. It shows two PET scans of the same slice of the same person's brain during the same task, four weeks apart. Everything is held as constant as possible, but there is a difference. In the left scan the subject was just beginning to learn to play the computer game Tetris; on the right, he or she had acquired considerable skill after a month of practice. The dramatic contrast in brightness between the left and right scans may reflect the fact that people are conscious of novel tasks in much greater detail than they are of the same task when it has become automatic. In other words, in these brain images we may be looking at the effects of different degrees of consciousness in playing Tetris. The two brain scans, side by side in close experimental comparison, provide a helpful image of the method of *contrastive phenomenology.*

If we could zoom in on one individual neuron, located in a single bright spot on the left scan, we would see the nerve cell communicating frantically to its neighbors about one thousand times per second, and taking in a continuous flow of input from others along its ten thousand dendrites. Local blood capillaries are expanding to service the increased energy needs of the cell, with oxygen and glucose being ferried rapidly to the spot and metabolic wastes flowing away in a ceaseless stream. Star-shaped glial support cells actually walk to the sites of neural activity to dispose of damaged cells.

PET scans reflect the blood flow carrying nutrients to nerve cells, and the more active the cells, the greater the local blood flow tends to be. In this case, the subject was injected just before the PET scan with a solution of a glucose isotope, which emits positrons over a period of thirty to forty minutes. Active nerve cells use more glucose, so that greater concentrations of positrons signal greater metabolic activity.

The subject's head is surrounded by a gigantic steel drum containing positron detectors. A positron hit on a detector triggers a small voltage whose location is noted and sent to a powerful computer, which summarizes the concentration of positron emissions on a numerical map, and then constructs a precise three-dimensional model of the living brain in arbitrary pseudocolors—the colors you see in the brain scan— so that we can later select any desired slice of the brain and study it in detail. Bright colors symbolize high metabolic activity and thus high neural activity; dull colors stand for lower activity.

One hypothesis, then, is that the left scan is brighter because the subject is just learning to play Tetris, that he or she is therefore conscious of many more details of the game; increased consciousness may mean greater neural activity. While we always need to consider alternative hypotheses, one reasonable explanation of the difference between the two sides is that we are seeing a drop in conscious access to the details of Tetris. The right-hand brain scan is so much duller in color because there is less conscious activity.

For an isolated piece of evidence like this there are of course other explanations. Perhaps the left scan reflects greater *effort* on the part of the subject, rather than more conscious involvement. Maybe new experiences involve more widespread neural activity, independent of consciousness. Maybe the neural code changes between new and old skills. Perhaps there is a change in the location of neural activity between the left and right scans. In fact, there is evidence for several of these ideas.

The most important point for us here is that *the consciousness hypothesis is clearly testable*. That is the critical step. Now suppose we find, as we will see to an extent later in this book, that

1. Sensory areas that are conscious during some task always show more metabolic activity.
2. Paying attention to one thing rather than another involves greater neural firing.
3. Supraliminal compared to subliminal stimulation causes more brain activity as well.

We will then have several converging sources of information to support the hypothesis that *consciousness generally involves increased neural activity, compared to unconscious control conditions*. We can then conclude tentatively that consciousness appears to be associated with increased brain activity, and look for more evidence

4. In cases of brain damage in which people lose conscious access to some event that is still represented in the brain;
5. In situations in which there are two identical streams of processed input, but people are conscious of only one;
6. In situations in which there is hypnotically suggested perceptual blocking.

Do you see where we are going? The basic strategy is to test the difference between very similar conscious and unconscious brain processes, so that over more and more cases the consciousness hypothesis can become weaker or stronger. It is the notion of contrastive phenomenology that is key here. It does not *guarantee* an answer to the historic questions about consciousness because science does not come with guarantees. It does give us a way to test the real world for a real answer.

Once we can treat consciousness as a variable like all the others, teasing out the most plausible story becomes only a matter of normal science. It is never easy, and it is certainly not a foregone conclusion that consciousness will turn out to be the critical difference between the left and right scan in Insert 1. But even today, we can say that it is most unlikely that consciousness is *unrelated* to learning and automaticity, because of the consistent phenomenological evidence, as we shall see next.

Demonstration: The "Phenomenology" in Contrastive Phenomenology

To remind ourselves of the different *subjective experiences* we have during skilled and unskilled performance of the same task, we need only observe ourselves in the act of reading. At this instant your eyes are jumping and fixating, jumping and fixating in a purposeful fashion from one informative phrase on this line to the next, and you are effortlessly identifying letters and words, probably carrying on some inner speech, and encoding the letters on the page into abstract meanings, all within a second or so. To compare that virtuoso performance to the same experience when it is novel, we need only turn this book upside-down and read the next paragraph. Go ahead and do it.

What do you notice? Well, if you are like me you will become conscious of many details of reading that are normally quite unconscious.

You will have trouble telling the difference between letters like *n* and *u*; *m* and *w*; and *d, p, q,* and *b*. You will soon learn to use the surrounding context of each letter to decide if the word is "deer," "peer," or "beer." You will consciously wonder, is that word "quite" or "paint"? Well, it can't be a *q* if it is not followed by a *u*, so it must be a *p*. All this conscious thinking will get in the way of understanding the *meaning* of this paragraph, so you will slow down quite a lot from your ordinary reading speed. You may be talking to yourself more than usual, to stay focused on the letters and words. If we could take a PET scan of your brain at this moment, we should see much more intense activity than if you were to read this paragraph as usual, right side up.

This is what we mean by contrastive phenomenology. The key is to compare two active brain processes that are similar in most ways but differ in respect to consciousness. When the game Tetris has become nearly automatic, it is still Tetris; when you read the paragraph above upside down, you are still reading the same material. Granted that there are some other differences, such as slower reading speed and the like, these differences are not likely to explain the robust fact that automatic reading is unconscious in many respects but that it becomes conscious when it is turned into a novel task.

Contrastive analysis does not give an instantaneous answer to our questions about consciousness. It does allow us to ask that question in an empirically sensible way, just as we do anywhere else in science. It is not the last step on the path to an answer, but it could be the first.

Comparing Conscious and Unconscious Qualia

Many philosophers claim that "qualia," the subjective qualities of perception and imagery, are the most profoundly puzzling aspects of human experience. That includes colors, textures, shapes, the warm intensity of a musical chord or the compact purity of a trumpet call. It is hard to imagine how one could explain those conscious qualities, or even what it would mean to engage in such explanation. Surely the firing patterns of nerve cells do not explain the experience of royal blue velvet?

The cognitive linguist George Lakoff has given a counterargument to the idea that sensory qualities are impossible to explain. He suggests that we can carry out phenomenological contrasts even with qualitative experiences like color. Surely an artist working feverishly on an oil painting is conscious of colors and shapes, but not of that moment a week ago when an odd contrast between a light purple swath of cloth and its pale yellow surround captured his or her imagination.

wrong! reconstructed memories experiences does not imply that there is qualia before attempting to reconstruct.

Yet those moments of past contemplation shape our consciousness in the present—unconsciously, of course. There must therefore be "unconscious qualia"; the artist must be able to recall that particular shade of purple from memory, where it rested unconsciously for weeks or months; and the process of mixing paints to obtain just the right hue must be partly automatic. Otherwise how could that particular color be remembered and mixed just at the moment it is needed? And if there are unconscious representations of qualia, it follows that we can, in principle, compare matched conscious and unconscious qualia.

The existence of unconscious sensory qualities does not mean that we have *explained* the experience of a musical chord played on a piano, but rather that we can now put the question in a testable way. If we can understand the *difference* between conscious and unconscious knowledge of a C-major chord, we will have achieved something like an explanation of that unique and inimitable resonance.

The Two-Channel Experiment: A Primary Source of Evidence about Consciousness

In *two-channel experiments* people receive two dense streams of information sufficiently different that they cannot be fused into a single conscious flow. Two narratives will do, one in the left ear and the other in the right, or two fast ball games projected on a single video screen, say football and basketball. Under these circumstances the brain is compelled to select just one stream of information for consciousness. If the stream we are conscious of makes sense, the competing one will be unconscious. The two-channel experiment provides dozens of revealing opportunities to study the conscious and unconscious flows and the interaction between them. It is one of our most productive source of evidence about conscious *contents*.

Two-channel experiments began decades ago with experiments by British psychologist Donald E. Broadbent and others, in which subjects were asked to listen to two spoken stories, one in each ear, and to *shadow* one of them. Shadowing simply means repeating each word immediately as it is heard, like a shadow following a strolling pedestrian on a sunny day. Most dual-channel research has been done with auditory streams of information, but to give you an actual experience of these phenomena here, we will use visual examples. Ideally the words below would be presented by computer, one word at a time, at a fixed point in the middle of a screen. We will be a little more primitive technically and ask your brain to do the work for us.

Let's start with a familiar poem for the conscious stream. Please read the capitalized words below, out loud if you can, at a fairly brisk pace. Ignore the words in small letters:

Example A

MARY paper HAD A brick cream LITTLE LAMB morning ITS FLEECE day brick WAS dot WHITE flower fork AS SNOW, brick gem AND frog EVERY-WHERE front brick THAT MARY home house ink WENT knife brick THE LAMB milk WAS SURE lily car TO GO.

For convenience we can call the capitalized words the *primary stream*, and the lowercase words the *secondary stream*.

This method works best if you can read the primary stream of words as quickly as you can, without losing track of its meaning. If you were conscious of some intruding lowercase words, try reading the primary stream more quickly, until you are clearly aware of one stream and not the other.

Whenever my students and I try this demonstration at an adequate pace we seem to lose access to the lowercase words quite rapidly. Did you realize that "brick" was repeated in the secondary stream four different times? If not, you were probably less conscious of the secondary words. In careful experiments using auditory streams, one to each ear, Donald Norman has found that the *same* word repeated thirty-five times in the unconscious ear could not be recalled immediately afterward.

Behaviorism was still dominant when two-channel listening was first explored by Donald Broadbent, and at the time, this very revealing technique was never thought of as a tool for studying *consciousness*. "Consciousness" was simply not a defined term. Many researchers still think of these powerful effects as if they reflect only *selection,* not consciousness. From our point of view they show both; there is selection in deciding to listen to one ear or to read only capitalized words, and as a result the selected stream of information becomes conscious—as you know from your own experience. We have a formal test: Does the "attended stream" allow you to make accurate reports about your experience? If so, by common practice it is considered to be conscious.

Now we can easily experiment with different properties of the two streams and observe some of their brain effects. A unified experience depends on many factors, including some in the secondary stream. Try for instance to read only the *lowercase words* in Example A. What is the difference between focusing on the primary and secondary

stream? Which way do you get more intrusions? Because the secondary stream contains only disconnected words, people in such
experiments commonly report more difficulty maintaining a single
conscious focus. Consciousness has a great preference for predictable
structure over time.

What if there is no visual difference between the two streams? Let's
try to turn both streams into capitals. Try the following example, at the
same brisk pace as before.

Example B

MARY PAPER HAD A BRICK CREAM LITTLE LAMB MORNING ITS FLEECE
DAY PARTY WAS DOT WHITE FLOWER FORK AS SNOW, GARDEN GEM AND
FROG FRONT EVERYWHERE BOX THAT MARY HOME HOUSE INK WENT
KNIFE LETTER THE LAMB MILK WAS SURE LILY CAR TO GO.

It seems awfully hard to hang on to the primary stream without visible
help from print size. But is it just a matter of the visible letters? What if
we keep the visible distinction between the capitalized and lowercase
flow, but scramble the words of "Mary Had a Little Lamb"? Let's try it.

Example C

WAS paper SNOW A brick AND cream SURE morning ITS day HAD brick
WAS dot WHITE flower THE fork MARY, brick AS gem LITTLE frog GO front
brick MARY home FLEECE house TO ink LAMB knife THAT brick LAMB
milk EVERYWHERE lily car WENT.

Evidently the *structure and cohesion* of the conscious stream is also
an important factor. This is a basic finding about conscious experience.
As a rule, *anything* that helps us to maintain a sense of coherence in
the conscious stream also tends to keep the two streams separate and
distinct. When the primary stream coheres well, the secondary one is
shut out quite effectively.

Given a convenient experimental technique we can explore all the
variables we can think of. We can compare *saying* "Mary had a little
lamb" to *singing* it. (Which do you think will work better?) You can
change the incentives people have to separate the two channels, compare younger and older people, and look for the effects of specific
themes and contents.

What about the meaning level of language? Let's see if we change
the wording a little bit without altering the meaning substantially. . . .

Example D

MARY paper OWNED brick cream A BABY LAMB morning WITH PALE day
WOOL, brick WHEN dot SHE flower brick WALKED gem frog ANYWHERE
front brick THE SMALL home house ink ANIMAL knife brick CAME milk
AFTER lily car HER.

That seems to slow things quite a bit. But now let's change the
meaning even more, so that the conscious stream becomes less predictable.

Example E

JOHN paper STOLE A brick cream GIANT LLAMA, morning ITS FUR hat ink
room WAS SOILED brick AND SMELLY. brick WHEN dot THE ANIMAL part
RAN block lily ANYWHERE, jewel THE STRAPPING spoon YOUNG flower
fork MAN, brick HAD TO gem frog PURSUE front brick THE SILLY home
house ink BEAST HOME.

Obviously we could now experiment with Jabberwocky speech (no
real words at all, just syntax and function words), and any number of
other variables. Much evidence already exists along these lines. We will
refer to it throughout this book.

Is the unconscious stream simply shut out of the nervous system?
Apparently not. Although words from the unattended stream cannot be
reported, there are several indications that they can still be processed
unconsciously. Thirty years ago Neville Moray found that the sound of
one's own name in the unconscious stream will break through to consciousness. Other highly significant events, like the sound of a baby
crying in the night, will do the same.

Here is an illustration.

Example F

MARY paper HAD A cream, danger! LITTLE LAMB fire! help! ITS FLEECE
day, fear! WAS alarm! WHITE bomb! fork AS SNOW, scare! gem AND scan-
dal! EVERYWHERE (your name) brick THAT MARY home, house, ink WENT
knife, brick THE LAMB milk WAS SURE lily TO GO.

You get the idea. It is a simple effect, but it has important theoretical
implications. It shows, for example, that unconscious word processing
is not superficial; unconsciously we probably analyze sound, word identity, meaning, and personal significance. How else could the brain

detect the significance of the unconscious information before it interrupts the stream of consciousness?

While this "breakthrough" effect for significant unconscious stimuli has been known for many years, there are still many unanswered questions. Will *new* combinations break through to consciousness? We might think not; but we can actually test the matter with a little bit of work. It is easy to find two-word combinations that are emotionally evocative when they are combined, but not separately. For example, "eat" followed by "dirt," "drink" by "acid," or "drop" by "baby." Do these new word combinations break through to consciousness? If single alarming words can break through, but novel pairs of words do not, we may have learned something significant about conscious and unconscious mental processes.

Or suppose you want to test a hypothesis about unconscious personality influences. Psychoanalysts maintain that certain unconscious thoughts are alarming for one kind of person, but not for others. Lloyd A. Silverman and Howard Shevrin have advanced claims about subliminal messages with highly personal content; for example, schizophrenics are said to feel more relaxed and calm after subliminal presentation of "Mommy and I are one." These words are said to lead to a temporary reduction in symptoms.

Such claims are controversial but not untestable. Suppose we ask someone who suffers from a fear of heights to listen to a conscious sentence such as "I saw a tiny car in the street below," and simultaneous with the last word "below" present the word "fall" in the secondary ear. Would "fall," which evokes the fear of falling from a height, tend to break through to consciousness, as a baby's cry in the night will wake up its parents? If we wanted to test a conflict hypothesis about personal guilt as a cause of phobia, would the unconscious word "guilt" tend to break through? These questions can be tested easily with such methods.

The cognitive psychologist Donald G. MacKay has discovered even subtler influences from the unconscious stream. Most words in English have more than one meaning; a great part of understanding speech is deciding which meaning of an ambiguous word is the right one in some particular context. Can unconscious input influence conscious word interpretation? In a classic experiment, MacKay presented a sentence like "John and Mary were walking by the bank" in the conscious channel. One set of subjects received a series of words in the unconscious channel, designed so that "money" would be presented unconsciously just as the word "bank" occurred on the conscious side. A comparison group received "water" instead of "money." Question:

Would the conscious word "bank" be swayed by the simultaneous unconscious word? As it turns out, "money" shifted the conscious interpretations to "financial institution," while "water" moved it toward "river bank."

Notice that MacKay's finding is quite different from unconscious "breakthroughs" into the conscious stream. When a baby's cry breaks through to consciousness, it interrupts other thoughts. But in MacKay's experiment the conscious flow is never interrupted; only the *meaning* of ambiguous words seems to shift. Evidently there is deep language processing going on, on the unconscious side, since sound, word identity, and meaning must be understood before the conscious meaning of "bank" can be swayed.

Notice that these interactions of conscious and unconscious goings-on suggest a mind that is not divided into two isolated boxes, one called "Conscious" and the other "Unconscious." A naïve reading of Freud might suggest that in his thertory conscious and unconscious events are quite separate and do not interact on a continuing basis. The cognitive unconscious that emerges from these experiments is quite different. Rather than acting like two separate boxes, the two sides of the mind interact ceaselessly, like some Jamesian stream whose course is continuously shaped by unconscious rocks, banks, shoals, and trenches, invisible but powerful.

In sum, the two-channel experiment is simple, convenient, and revealing. It allows us to manipulate both the conscious and the unconscious streams, and to study their interaction. Only a fraction of its possibilities have been explored to date. Far more remains to be done with this method, which may be the most practical way to study contrastive phenomenology today.

Consciousness as a State: Wakefulness and Coma

Another major source of phenomenal contrasts comes from comparing waking consciousness with deep sleep and coma. Such comparisons show that waking consciousness is not some vague or fuzzy feature of the brain. An astonishing amount of brain tissue can be lost from the great cerebral hemispheres without abolishing the state of consciousness, while tiny lesions in the slender axial core of the brain cause irreversible coma. We have known since the 1950s that a small area in the brain stem called the *reticular formation* is necessary for waking consciousness (see Figure 1-1). When people with head injuries go into coma, it is often because tissue damage at the front of the head causes widespread swelling, choking off the blood supply even to the brain stem. When oxygen supply is lost to the reticular formation the result is coma; and because the nerve centers that control breathing and heart action are located very nearby, death often follows.

It has now become clear that a second part of the core brain is required for waking consciousness; it is located an inch or so above the reticular formation, in the central transfer station of the brain, the thalamus.

The case of Karen Ann Quinlan caused headlines some years ago as a dramatic example of loss of consciousness *without* loss of vital functions like breathing and heartbeat, a type of coma called *persistent vegetative state*. Karen Quinlan, a young woman in her twenties, lost consciousness after suffering cardiac arrest, followed by a stroke that blocked the flow of oxygen to her midbrain in a catastrophically precise fashion. Given the rather barbaric state of our medical ethics, her family was confronted with the choice either to leave her on life support for an indefinite future or to allow her to starve slowly to death. Newspapers headlined the story for years while the case dragged through the courts until at last, mercifully perhaps, she was allowed to die.

Postmortem analysis of Karen Quinlan's brain has now been published in the *New England Journal of Medicine,* showing that the crucial damage involved the loss of quite a small part of each thalamus. Additional damage was found, but in regions that do not seem to affect consciousness directly (Kinney et al., 1994).

Imagine a giant dome divided into two equal halves, the two cerebral hemispheres (Figure 1-1). Each half dome has an egg-shaped body lying on one side of the midline. That is the thalamus, truly a minibrain within the brain. The major centers of the thalamus, the nuclei, make up a microcosm of the great hemispheres, each one intimately connected with a corresponding area of cortex. On the sensory side, each nucleus mirrors the sensory cortex, and on the output side, each one reflects the motor cortex. So intimately are thalamic centers bound up with corresponding areas of cortex that the prefrontal cortex is anatomically defined as those parts of the frontal cortex that are connected with the forward nucleus of each thalamus.

Now imagine great fiber cables flowing inward from the eyes, the ears, and the skin, to major relay centers in the two egg-shaped thalami. On emerging, they radiate in elegant wings of cell fibers to the sensory cortex, located on the surface of each half dome—vision at the rear, touch on top, and hearing on the side of each hemisphere. Motor

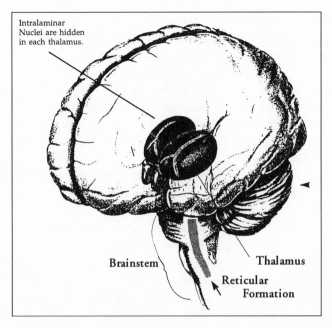

Intralaminar
Nuclei are hidden
in each thalamus.

Brainstem   Thalamus

Reticular
Formation

Figure 1-1 *The thalamus is a relay station to cortex.* The two *thalami*, one
for each hemisphere, contain relay connections for the major input and
output tracts of the brain. All sensory channels (except smell) stop off at
large neural centers in each thalamus before going up to the sensory areas
of the cortex for analysis. The two thalami are therefore strategically
located for directing traffic to and from the cortical centers—the function of selective attention. Notice that the major divisions of each thalamus are separated by white layers of tissue, called the *laminae*. Tucked
inside pockets in the laminae are the *intralaminar nuclei*, clumps of
nerve cells about the size of a pencil eraser. The ILN clusters are deeply
implicated in the workings of waking consciousness. They trigger the cortical EEG characteristic of wakefulness. Damage to both ILNs leads to
irreversible coma, even massive damage in the cortex does not lead to a
loss of consciousness. From Neil R. Carlson, *Physiology of Behavior 4/E.*
Copyright © 1991 by Allyn and Bacon. Reprinted/adapted by permission.

tracts flow the other way, coming down from cortex, stopping off in
each thalamus, and then going out to the muscles.

To complete the picture, take a close look at each thalamic egg and
notice that deep inside, sandwiched between the massive transfer stations for the sensory and motor tracts, are a few small structures, these
small islands are called the intralaminar nuclei (ILN) because they fit
inside the *laminae*, the layers of white tissue that separate the major
thalamic nuclei. Neurons in each set of ILN send a fine, widely pro-

jecting spray of fibers to all parts of the great cortical dome above. Through these fibers the ILN cells trigger *cortical arousal,* the distinctive electrical signature of waking consciousness.

Neurosurgeon and researcher Joseph Bogen has pointed out that damage to both right and left ILN causes complete coma, indicating that the two sets of intralaminar nuclei constitute a *necessary condition* for waking consciousness (Bogen, 1995). Aside from the reticular formation, this is the only part of the brain that seems indispensible for waking consciousness.

Karen Quinlan's great misfortune was to fall victim to a stroke that blocked the blood supply to *both* ILN clusters on either side of the brain. Loss of the intralaminar nuclei on one side can be sustained, sometimes with temporary coma; we can be conscious with just one healthy side, just as we can breathe with only one lung. But damage to both sets of intralaminar nuclei does occur because, by some great flaw in the brain's design, a single artery in the center of the brain divides in two to supply life-giving oxygen to *both* ILNs on either side of the midline. If that single artery is interrupted before it divides in two, both sets of intralaminar nuclei may die for lack of oxygen. A stroke at this strategic junction can wreak havoc very quickly: several minutes of low oxygen may cause irreversible damage. Bogen estimates that the area of fatal damage to either ILN need be no bigger than a pencil eraser.

A dramatic comparison can be made between two kinds of brain damage, one in the core brain (the ILN and the reticular core of the brain stem), and the other in the massive cortical mantle that wholly covers the core brain. There is a fairly common operation called a *hemispherectomy,* which involves removal of an entire hemisphere— half of the cortex. It is a drastic measure, but when a tumor has deeply invaded one side of the brain, cutting out the whole hemisphere can save the patient's life. Hemispherectomies drastically affect the contents of consciousness on the side of the cut, though some function is taken up by the other side. *But as massive as they are, they do not lead to coma.*

In sum, losing tiny areas in the core of the brain leads to a loss of waking consciousness, and massive damage elsewhere does not. This is exactly the kind of "contrastive case" that allows us to think about consciousness as a variable. Consciousness is not some fuzzy or indeterminable business at the level of the brain. It requires the small ILN centers and the reticular formation in the core of the brain stem.

There are many unanswered questions. What do the ILN clusters do? Many neuroscientists believe that the fibers emerging from the ILN to the cortex seem too sparse to support a full, conscious experience of a symphony orchestra or a cheering football stadium. One hypothesis is that the ILN works with another small nucleus, the reticular nucleus, to generate a regular waveform about forty times per second, which may serve to coordinate and "bind" many specific areas of cortex into a single, conscious experience. Neuroscientist Rodolfo Llinás has become a major advocate of this hypothesis. A related idea is that these signals may facilitate reentrant loops, cycling back and forth between the sensory cortex and the relay stations of the thalamus, looping and building on itself until its activity rises above a threshold of conscious activity and drowns out the uncoordinated firing of other neurons. Such a coherent reentrant loop may correspond to a conscious experience, according to Nobelist Gerald Edelman and others (Edelman, 1989). Both the forty-hertz hypothesis and the reentrant loop notion may be true. They are viable hypotheses, which do not yet command a consensus. They may be definitively accepted or rejected over the next few years.

We are always half-ignorant, of course, never yet at the point where we understand the most interesting issues. But we now know enough, I believe, to narrow down the possibilities; even to make firm claims about some of the long-standing debates. Among those is the question of animal consciousness.

Are Animals Conscious?

Just to illustrate how clearly the evidence has begun to accumulate on some hotly debated issues, consider the question of animal consciousness. It has raged for centuries, from Aristotle's proclamation that animals have a kind of soul (hence the word "animal," from *anima*, soul) to Descartes's more restrictive view that our animal cousins are merely automata. We know that the brain evolved cumulatively, each new layer on top of ancestral layers that are mostly unchanged. All vertebrates have brain stems, required for wakefulness; all mammals have sizable midbrains on top of the brain stem, containing the thalamus and its ILN clusters, another requirement for waking consciousness; and all mammals have perceptual cortex, mushrooming over these older structures, which we need to experience sensory consciousness (Figure 1-2).

Now let us forget for a moment our self-serving wish to have our own species stand out as utterly different from other animals. Pretend to observe life on earth with the cold gaze of a visitor from another star system. What do you notice about consciousness?

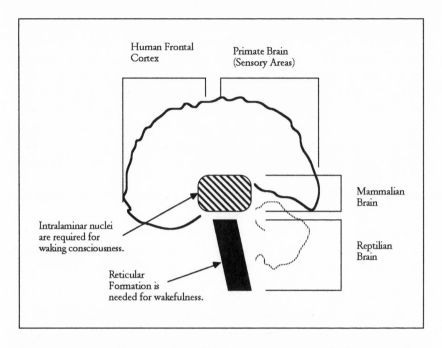

Figure 1-2. *Animals are very probably conscious.* This is shown not just by their actions but also by the anatomy of the brain. The brain stem is sometimes called the "reptilian brain" because its basic features are shared by reptiles; it contains an ancient structure called the *reticular formation* which is indispensable to waking consciousness. Likewise, the midbrain is essentially the "mammalian brain"; it includes the *thalamus*, with nuclei that are also crucial for maintaining consciousness. By contrast, the cortex is not needed for the state of waking consciousness but shapes the contents of conscious experience. The rapid evolutionary growth of the cortex comes with primates, starting about five million years ago. Humans differ from our primate cousins mainly in our greatly expanded frontal cortex. It seems therefore that basic waking and sensory consciousness are shared with other species.

Only one species on earth is *articulate* about its experience, having devoted the last two millennia to writing about it. Yet the brain anatomy that supports the *state* of consciousness in this most talkative species can also be found in other mammals. The brain stem centers involved with sleep, wakefulness, and emergency wake-up calls are much the same in our brains as they were in ancestral reptilia, and the resulting electrical activity of the brain looks identical. Species closer to us, including all mammals and birds, have the mid brain thalamus in addition to the reptilian brain stem. As for sensory cortex, the visual cortex in macaque monkeys resembles the human visual brain so closely that macaques are routinely studied to gather information about human vision. Thus *perceptual consciousness* appears to be quite similar in monkeys, apes, and humans. Dogs and cats lack color vision, but they probably have a more acute sense of smell.

Nor are our waking activities utterly different from other animals. All animals engage in purposeful action when their brains show the electrical activity of waking or seeking food, mates, and the company of others. All mammals snarl when threatened and writhe when wounded, and while we cannot tell directly whether they relish eating, any pet owner can testify to the frenzied excitement of hungry dogs and cats before a meal, their apparent eagerness to eat, and all the signs of lazy satisfaction afterwards. Animals seem to work as hard as humans do to obtain food when hungry, and sexual contact when in heat. All mammalian mothers protect and suckle their young, and both sexes engage in the eternal dance of mate selection. Other animals investigate novel and biologically significant stimuli as we do, ignore old and uninteresting events just as we do, and share our limited capacity for incoming information.

Do animals show all the observable aspects of consciousness? The biological evidence points to a clear yes. Are they then likely to have the subjective side as well? Given the long and growing list of similarities, the weight of evidence, it seems to me, is inexorably moving toward yes.

Is there still controversy about animal consciousness? My sense is that the scientific community has now swung decisively in its favor. The basic facts have come home at last. We are not the only conscious beings on earth.

Human Uniqueness

Human beings *are* different of course. We have mastered spoken language, a single biological adaptation that is crucial for human culture, technology, and mass society. Indeed, humans seem to spend most of our waking hours silently talking to ourselves. We also come equipped with a uniquely large frontal cortex, useful for long-term planning, abstract thought, and voluntary executive functions. Purposeful use of mental imagery is likely to be limited to humans. All these uniquely human capacities make use of consciousness, even as they extend its reach. Human consciousness seems to differ from that of other animals both in its *contents* and in its capacities, such as our ability to pay long-term, purposeful attention over months or years to a remotely apprehended purpose—that is, to control what we are conscious of in pursuit of long-term goals.

But we can no longer pose absolute barriers between ourselves and other animals. As always in this Age of Darwin, we must come to terms with the fact that we are half animal, half human. The Cartesian notion that humans are the only conscious species flies in the face of the evidence.

We can already see some clear results from contrastive phenomenology. Some of these results may not sit well with some critics. But that is not a *scientific* problem. The science speaks for itself.

But Is It the Real Thing?

Some philosophers maintain that the experiential descriptions we have collected in a century of sensory science may *parallel* conscious experience without actually resulting from it. Prominent philosophers of science like Ned Block of MIT have recently advanced arguments of this kind. But this seems utterly implausible to an empirical scientist. If the overwhelming majority of people say a pencil is red, if they can match it with other red things and distinguish it from blue and green pencils; if their eyes have red receptors, and color cells in the visual cortex fire a red code, what else would they be having but a conscious experience of red?

There may always be those who maintain that what we learn from contrastive phenomenology has nothing to do with real consciousness. The best reply I can think of is to ask skeptics to try one of the demonstrations in this chapter, and ask, *is this truly your experience?* If yes, an honest skeptic should say that we are indeed dealing with genuine consciousness as a valid topic for exploration.

Could the evidence regarding consciousness just be a clever imitation of the real thing? Such arguments remind me of Darwin's most adamant critics, who after many years of debate proposed that God created the geological fossil record merely to test our faith. It was a last, desperate move against the evolutionary hypothesis. As an answer, we need only notice that *consciousness as an object of scientific scrutiny fits our personal experience remarkably well.* That is not likely to be a coincidence.

In sum, do we have hard evidence bearing on conscious experience?
  Yes.

Further Reading

Readers interested in philosophical issues may want to read Owen Flanagan's *Consciousness Reconsidered* (1992), one of the clearest overviews of a complex field. A more advanced view is given by John Searle in *The Rediscovery of the Mind* (1900), by Daniel Dennett in *Consciousness Explained* (1991), and by David Chalmers' The Conscious Mind (1996). There are many excellent philosophy books, but most advance a specific, controversial point of view, so that a newcomer will obtain only one of several perspectives.

Good introductions to the brain processes involved in conscious experience are provided by Francis H. C. Crick in *The Astonishing Hypothesis: The Scientific Search for the Soul* (1993), and by Robert Ornstein and Richard F. Thompson in *The Amazing Brain* (1993). William H. Calvin and George A. Ojemann have written an excellent account from the perspective of a brain surgeon in *Conversations with Neil's Brain* (1994).

A more advanced effort is Gerald M. Edelman's *The Remembered Present: A Biological Theory of Consciousness* (1989). Recent breakthroughs in brain imagery are showcased in a remarkable work called *Imaging the Brain*, written by two wonderful scientific pioneers, Michael Posner and Marcus Raichle (1994). It has extraordinary snapshots of brain activity during simple mental tasks, now available for the first time in history based on PET scans.

Remarkably, the best source on the psychology of consciousness is still William James's Elegant *Principles of Psychology*, first published in 1890, but never out of print. His *Psychology: The briefer Course* (1893) is a short introduction based on the thirteen hundred pages of the great work. James's thought must be understood in historical context, but the phenomena he describes so well have not changed one bit.

Part II

A UNIFIED IMAGE

We have so much evidence today about conscious experience that a single integrative image is helpful to keep it all in place. The theater metaphor of mind is both ancient and modern. Plato and Aristotle used it, as did the Vedanta philosophers and William James. Modern researchers who have developed scientific theater models include Herbert A. Simon, Allan Newell, and John R. Anderson in cognitive science, and Francis Crick in neurobiology. I. P. Pavlov referred to the "bright spot" in the cortex which integrated all sensory input into one united activity. All these views seem to reflect a similar set of insights. In this section we explore the scientific uses of the theater of consciousness.

THE THEATER STAGE
HAS *LIMITED CAPACITY*
BUT CREATES *VAST ACCESS*

Can this cockpit hold
The vasty fields of France? Or may we cram
within this wooden O the very casques
That did affright the air at Agincourt?
. . .
Piece out our imperfections with your thoughts;
. . .
Think, when we talk of horses, that you see them
Printing their proud hoofs i' th' receiving earth;
For 'tis your thoughts that now must deck our kings,
. . .
Turning th' accomplishment of many years
Into an hourglass.

—SHAKESPEARE, HENRY V, PROLOGUE

*L*et your eyes sweep along a great canvas, and the richness of detail may seem overwhelming. But to really "see" a fine painting we need to see it thoughtfully, many times. The reason is that the capacity of conscious contents at any single moment is surprisingly limited: we cannot read this sentence and listen to a conversation at the same time. Nor can we pay attention to the s-p-e-l-l-i-n-g of a word without taking a risk that we will miss some of its meaning.

In fact, our sensory systems pick up only a little bit of conscious information at any moment. If you close one eye and focus steadily on the following + sign in the line of numbers from about eight inches away, it becomes difficult to see the surrounding numbers. Try it, without letting your focus wander:

5   4   3   2   1   (+)   1   2   3   4   5

High-resolution vision uses the tiny patch of retina called the *fovea*, packed with light receptors, which we point at the world when we want to see something. The fovea is limited to about four degrees of visual arc—a tiny keyhole of clarity in a very fuzzy visual field. If you stretch out your arm in front and hold up two fingers, they will subtend about four degrees of visual arc. We all have the illusion of seeing far more because the brain cleverly takes foveal snapshots of high-information regions in the visual scene and fills in the rest with plausible guesswork.

Take another look at the last word in the previous paragraph, "guesswork": you can become conscious of it with a single foveal glance. It is one of about one hundred thousand words in your recognition vocabulary. Though "guesswork" is a relatively rare word, most readers will grasp its meaning in a fraction of a second. Merely being conscious of a target word seems to trigger a search through a mental lexicon to access its meaning; but *the process of* searching the lexicon is of course unconscious. Once aware of its meaning we immediately gain access to many other abilities; we can define "guesswork," generate paraphrases, and distinguish it from subtly different words. The details of these abilities are of course unconscious. We can also use the word in an endless array of grammatical sentences, control the high-speed movements of hundreds of muscles in the vocal tract that are needed to pronounce it, and detect errors at any level, including spelling, pronunciation, and usage. In sum, conscious access to a tiny visual keyhole allows "guesswork" to become conscious, one lonely little word out of hundreds on this page; but that brief event creates immediate access to a vast world of knowledge. The payoff for limited capacity seems to be vast access.

Consciousness is the private arena in which we live our lives. Many of us maintain a coherent narrative, some framework in which growing up, adulthood and old age make up the parts of a meaningful tale. Traditional cultures provide plot patterns for such stories, opening and closing doors that every male and female is expected to encounter, with ceremonial rites of passage to tell the story to the clan. Our inner life narrative seems to happen within some such framework, even though modern culture creates far fewer occasions to give a symbolic accounting of oneself to a chorus of public witnesses. Sometimes we seem to address an inner jury instead.

Here is a version of the theater model that allows us to think about the evidence in a unified way. Imagine entering a theater just before the beginning of the show, noticing the stage, the chatting audience, and a few side doors leading backstage. As the house lights begin to dim and the audience falls silent, a single spotlight pierces the descending darkness, until only one bright spot, shining on stage, remains visible. You know that the audience, actors, stagehands, and spotlight operators are there, working together under invisible direction and guided by an unknown script, to present the flow of visible events on stage. As the house lights dim, only the focal contents of consciousness remain. Everything else is in darkness. Consider Figure 2-1 on the next page.

1. *Working memory is like a theater stage.* All unified models of the mind have a small "working memory" that is closely associated with conscious processes. Working memory is that inner domain in which we can rehearse telephone numbers to ourselves or, more interestingly, in which we carry on the narrative of our lives. It is usually thought to include *inner speech* and *visual imagery.*

Inner speech is what you hear yourself saying while silently reading a difficult passage; or after a heated argument with a friend, when you remind yourself of all the good things you should have said but couldn't think of at the time. It has a *speaking* and a *hearing and comprehension* component. Verbal working memory appears to make use of the same parts of cortex that are involved in outer speaking and listening.

Visual imagery helps us to display and solve spatial problems. Most people use it spontaneously without realizing that they are doing so. If you try for a moment to imagine the streets you see coming home from work, and remind yourself to stop at the local grocery store to buy some milk for the cat . . . can you see it? That is the mind's eye. It, too, seems to involve the same parts of cortex we use to see the outer world.

Over the last few decades we have gathered a great body of solid evidence about the verbal and visual components of working memory, but one thing has not changed: Working memory is remarkably *limited.* We can keep seven unrelated items in the verbal part, and in the mind's eye perhaps four.

All working memories operate serially, one thing at a time. They show a *stream* of events, just as the spotlight shining on the stage of a theater may show each individual actor speaking to the audience, one at a time.

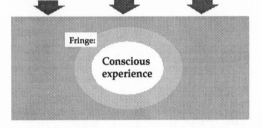

Context operators behind the scenes

Director | Spotlight Controller | Local Contexts

Competing for access to consciousness:

the players ...

Outer Senses
Seeing
Hearing
Feeling
Tasting
Smelling
Submodalities
Heat
Vibration

Inner Senses
Visual Imagery
Inner Speech
Dreams
Imagined
Feelings

Ideas
Imagible Ideas
Verbalized Ideas
Fringe Conscious
Intuitions.

... the spotlight of attention shining on the stage of working memory ...

Fringe:

Conscious experience

Working memory receives conscious input, controls inner speech, uses imagery for spatial tasks, all under voluntary control.

the unconscious audience...

Memory systems:

Lexicon
Semantic networks
Autobiographical
& declarative memory
Beliefs, knowledge
of the world, of
oneself and others.

Interpreting conscious contents:

Recognizing objects, faces, speech,
events. Syntactic analysis. Spatial
relationships. Social inferences.

Automatisms:

Skill memory.
Details of language,
action control, reading,
thinking, and
thousands more ...

Motivational systems:

Is the conscious event relevant to my goals?   Emotional responses, facial
expressions, preparing the body for action. Managing goal conflicts.

2. *The players onstage: the contents of conscious experience.* Consciousness shows *competition and cooperation* between different "players," the different sources of conscious experience that try to reach the stage. Listening to a conversation in a crowded party is one example. It is helpful at a loud party to combine visual and sound information by reading the lips of speakers you want to hear. This is a case of cooperation between two channels of information. But watch a film with a sound track lagging a half second behind an actor's mouth movements, and the eye and ear begin to compete. Only one of the two sources can win at any given moment. Our conscious experience is always a coherent mix of cooperating elements; incompatible input is simply excluded from consciousness.

Our capacity for conscious contents is radically small: essentially we can take in only one dense train of conscious contents at a time. Fortunately, we can pack a vast amount of information into that single flow of experience, and sometimes, as in talking to a friend while driving, we can jump back and forth between different streams.

The limited capacity of consciousness is one reason for the theater metaphor. Like other scientific analogies it allows us to package a large amount of evidence into a simple, organized image. As you read this book you may notice that your mental image of the theater of consciousness will become more and more densely packed and elaborated, but you will still be able to understand it as a unit.

Figure 2-1. *A theater metaphor for conscious experience.* All unified theories of cognition today involve theater metaphors. In this version, conscious contents are limited to a brightly lit spot of attention onstage, while the rest of the stage corresponds to immediate working memory. Behind the scenes are executive processes, including a director, and a great variety of contextual operators that shape conscious experience without themselves becoming conscious. In the audience are a vast array of intelligent unconscious mechanisms. Some audience members are automatic routines, such as the brain mechanisms that guide eye movements, speaking, or hand and finger movements. Others involve autobiographical memory, semantic networks representing our knowledge of the world, declarative memory for beliefs and facts, and the implicit memories that maintain attitudes, skills, and social interaction. Elements of working memory—on stage, but not in the spotlight of attention—are also unconscious. Notice that different inputs to the stage can work together to place an actor in the conscious bright spot, a process of *convergence*; but once on stage, conscious information *diverges*, as it is is widely disseminated to members of the audience. By far the most detailed functions are carried on outside of awareness.

3. *The spotlight of attention. Conscious contents emerge when the bright spotlight of attention falls on a player on the stage of working memory. But the spotlight has a fringe. . . .*

To illustrate, look at the following numbers carefully.

11, 23, 4, 61, 3, 17

Now close your eyes for about ten seconds, and then write the numbers down. What was conscious when you closed your eyes? Most people report that at any given moment, whatever number is *being said* in their inner speech is conscious; numbers that are momentarily not being said are not. There seems to be a clear phenomenological contrast between currently conscious and currently stored numbers. Try it a few times to see if you agree. If the results are reliable and if we can verify them independently, we generally take them to be valid.

The spotlight of attention has a crucial role in our version of the theater metaphor, for whenever it falls on some particular actor he or she comes to consciousness. Actors in the spotlight are privileged in the theater metaphor. They are the only ones who can disseminate information to an audience of specialized experts—who represent the unconscious resources of memory, knowledge, and automatic routines. The audience in turn may hiss or applaud, asking to hear more or less from any given actor. Audience members can also exchange information among themselves and form coalitions to bring other messages to the stage. But there is only one way to reach the audience as a whole, and that is by way of an actor in the spotlight on stage.

Imagine that the bright spot onstage is surrounded by a hazy penumbra, to represent a very interesting phenomenon that William James called *fringe consciousness*. If we take focal consciousness to include immediate, detailed experience, the fringe would cover those cases in which we have reliable access to information without being able to experience it explicitly in detail. Cognitive scientist Bruce Mangan has helped revive a long philosophical tradition about the fringe, including such experiences as feelings of knowing, familiarity, beauty, and goodness, of something not quite fitting, or a sudden profound feeling of rightness (Mangan, 1993). A surprising amount of our mental life is occupied with fringe events, which may be experienced as fuzzy or vague, but which have properties suggesting that something very precise is going on.

Take the "feeling of knowing" that comes when we ask a question like, *What is the name of the flying reptiles of the dinosaur age?* Most of us have trouble finding the answer right away, but we know that we know it, and rightly so. Feelings of knowing have been studied quite a bit, and the evidence indicates that (1) they are quite accurate most of the time; and (2) they receive high confidence ratings; but (3) they do not involve detailed, structured experiences, unlike the sight of a coffee cup, where we can talk about shape, color, shading, texture, and many other details.

We have feelings of knowing about items in working memory that are not currently conscious. Moreover, we seem to have feelings of knowing about things that are readily *available* to consciousness, though they are not conscious at the moment—our ability to find known words, our mood, our ability to act and control some mental functions, our basic knowledge about friends, relatives, and ourselves, and much more.

4. *Contexts operate behind the scenes to shape events onstage.* This point involves unconscious *contextual operators* that set the background against which the brightly lit actors play their roles. They are invisible behind the scenes but have profound effects on consciousness. Your experience at this moment is shaped by unconscious expectations about the syntax of this sentence, as well as by beliefs you may have formed ago about human consciousness. Context effects are ubiquitous and powerful.

Among these behind-the-scenes operators are a *director,* which performs executive functions—what William James called "the self as agent and observer." *We*—whoever *we* are—have voluntary control over parts of working memory. At times we can control what will come into consciousness next, and whether to redirect the current stream when something more urgent happens. Voluntary functions involve frontal cortex, and injury to frontal cortex often degrades executive control. (See Chapter 7).

Finally, we have

5. *The audience.* This is what it's all about; it is the raison d'être of the whole design. We do so many things unconsciously, and the neuronal networks that perform unconscious functions are so widely distributed throughout the brain, that the notion of a vast *society* of specialized systems has become very natural. If we think of the brain as a distributed system with millions of specialized abilities, the question becomes *how to mobilize all of the specialized unconscious networks in pursuit of survival and reproduction.* This is presumably why the unconscious society of the brain requires a stage, a spotlight, and a director. Consciousness, in this view, serves to disseminate a small amount of information to a vast unconscious audience in the brain. It is the publicity organ in the society of mind.

[margin note: consciousness is for resource management]

It is terribly important to keep in mind that audience members are merely metaphorical. Automatic routines tend to be relatively separate, specialized and autonomous; but in fact they work together with others to carry out the details of even the simplest action. Audience members, if you will, have a vast telephone network connecting each to each, enabling them to carry out routine tasks without consciousness. Consciousness is not needed for many of these routine collaborative activities; it seems to be needed for new combinations of ingredients. It is likely that today's routine collaborations between separate automatic units were created in the past with the help of consciousness; today's automatic processes emerged from yesterday's effortful and elaborately conscious projects.

All unified models of cognition today suggest some sort of unconscious audience, including unconscious memory archives and automatic routines that are triggered when their "calling conditions" appear in working memory. In the brain the audience seems to consist of functional networks and routines—collections of neurons that work together to perform some job. We can think of them as people sitting in the dark audience, unconscious but with great local expertise.

Some audience members specialize in memory, including the hunderd-thousand-word lexicon of English that you are using at this very moment; your autobiographical memory, a noisy record of a lifetime of conscious experiences; implicit memory, the patterns, skills, and regularities you have learned since birth; semantic memory, the knowledge that is needed to understand this paragraph; and declarative memory, which includes explicit beliefs about the world and oneself.

Here is an example of an unconscious, automatic process. Try to read the words below *without* saying them to yourself:

inchoate

Papa Doc

infundibulum

I cannot avoid sounding them in my inner speech, no matter how hard I try. The mere visual experience of the printed word seems to trigger auditory echoes. This is one example of the automatisms that control our delicate and purposeful eye movements, linguistic analyses, visual scene interpretation, bodily posture, and all the moment-to-moment inferences we make whenever we look or listen or try to understand anything.

In many ways the audience acts as a legislature. Some audience members may hiss or applaud certain messages from the stage, or build coalitions to help their favorite actors compete against others for access to the stage. Different goals may try to become conscious in a dynamic game of king of the hill, as we can guess by observing the ever-changing impulsive actions of young children. Over time, impulsive goals may eventually coalesce into working hierarchies that support more coherent and long-term actions. The adult self may involve a more settled version of the child's impulsive, short-term goals.

A great body of evidence can be understood in terms of these six basic ideas—the stage, the bright light of attention, actors and their speeches, the audience, contexts, and director. The actors in the spotlight may fret and strut their hour on the stage, cued by the director against a background created by contextual operators. The spotlight selects the most important events on stage, which are then distributed to an audience consisting of all the unconscious routines and knowledge sources in the hall.

These are the basic ingredients of the theater, a few ideas to limn a vast biological brain in broad outline. If our metaphor seems puny in the face of that immense reality, that is surely true. The question is, can this simple set of ideas capture some basic set of facts about human experience? Let us see.

Theater Diagrams

It is helpful to visualize new ideas, and the theater metaphor is no exception. We can show its essentials with a few lines and circles, allowing us to sketch out various ways in which the theater might work in the following chapters. Theater diagrams are simplicity itself. The stage is a small rectangle, with a small oval to symbolize the spotlight. Actors are shown as arrows going on stage. The contexts that operate backstage are simple horizontal brackets, and the audience is just a collection of little circles. If we want to see a stream of conscious events over time, we need only and draw a series of boxes with a time arrow, as shown in Figure 2-2.

Two different time scales are known to be important. Conscious perceptual integration is on the order of one-tenth of a second. If two identical pictures are presented to the two eyes more than one-tenth second apart, they will not fuse into a single image; but with time differences of less than one-tenth second, they are experienced as a whole. That scale is shown in the upper time arrow of Figure 2-2.

By contrast, working memory plays out on a scale of seconds, as you can tell simply by counting to yourself in inner speech. Various measures show the duration of working memory to be about ten seconds. This is the time scale on which we talk to ourselves and make thoughtful decisions. This more common-sense grain of experience is shown in the lower time arrow of Figure 2-2.

Notice, by the way, that today's neuroimaging techniques do not have the temporal resolution needed to show what is happening at these time scales, though improvements are coming so fast that we should be able to see brain activities over seconds, if not milliseconds, within a decade.

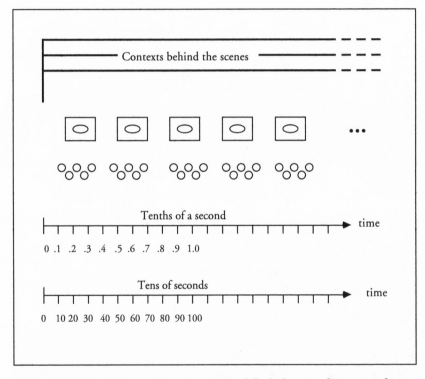

Figure 2-2. *Brief theater diagrams.* Simplified theater diagrams show a series of snapshots over time of the actors on stage, the audience, and contexts. Two time scales are of special importance. Sensory events occurring within a tenth of a second merge into a single conscious sensory experience, suggesting a 100-millisecond scale. But working memory, the domain in which we talk to ourselves or use our visual imagination, stretches out over roughly 10-second steps. The tenth-of-a-second level is automatic, while the 10-second level is shaped by conscious plans and goals.

Spontaneous Problem-Solving:
That Little Pause before the Answer Comes to Mind

Consider the following questions:

1. What is the name of a herbivorous dinosaur?
2. What technology develops artificial limbs?
3. What are three synonyms for "talkative"?

Did you experience a brief pause before the answers came to mind? (If you are not sure, try it one more time.) That brief "dead time" of simply waiting for the unconscious to do its job of finding the answer is typical of spontaneous problem solving. It starts with a conscious moment when the question is asked or the problem assigned; followed by some period of unconscious incubation; and ends with a return of the answer to consciousness. We certainly don't need to be deliberately trying to solve the problem. All we need is some incomplete _____ to start a problem-solving process.

Spontaneous problem-solving can cover lifetime issues, fantasies about the future, finding a memory of elementary school, control of one's own body, searching for the right word at the right time, understanding a sentence, trying to influence other people, and an endless variety of other things people think about.

Figure 2-3 shows a theater diagram for the principal elements of spontaneous problem-solving: conscious problem-priming, unconscious problem-solving, and conscious display of the solution. Or, if we want to be a little more complicated, we can show a goal that is achieved by way of a number of subgoals. This is much more realistic in cases like mental arithmetic; multiplying 324×11 has the subgoal of multiplying 324×10. Each subgoal seems to have the same three-stage format as a top-level goal.

Creative processes in art, science, and mathematics seem to show the same pattern of conscious assignment, unconscious processing, and conscious emergence of the answer. But so do short-term tasks like word search, question answering, the interpretation of ambiguous words, action control, and the like. The stream of consciousness may be created by the interplay of many goals, each tending to make conscious whatever will promote its progress. When all these spontaneous problem-solving patterns are intertwined, the stream of consciousness may *seem* random and without purpose. Researchers like Jerome Singer report that on closer examination spontaneous thought seems to be

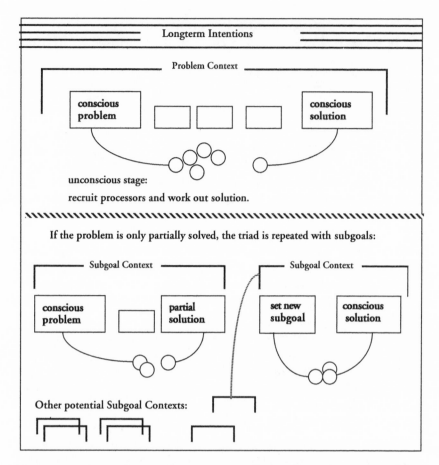

Figure 2-3. *Using theater diagrams to understand spontaneous problem solving.* **Most everyday problems are solved without specific step-by-step conscious procedures. Such spontaneous problem-solving characteristically involves three phases: conscious problem assignment, unconscious processing, and finally conscious display of the solution. It is a pattern that can occur over short intervals, as in memory retrieval, or over hours and days, as in mathematical problem solving. Most real problems, like mental arithmetic or chessplaying, have subgoals within the larger goal, which seem to repeat the three-stage pattern.**

concerned with many unresolved problems to which we return time and time again until we find a satisfying answer.

Notice how much trust we need in the competence and creativity of the unconscious. Chances are that unconscious incubation makes use of all the highly practiced automatisms that we have thought about consciously over our lifetimes. Word search is an unconscious type of problem solving in the mental lexicon, but it can include all the words we have paid attention to in our lives. It seems that the unconscious mechanisms that are quietly buzzing away before the answer is returned are themselves the working residues of earlier conscious thoughts.

The role of unconscious problem-solving was described a century ago by the mathematician Henri Poincaré, who devoted much thought to the psychology of mathematical creation. He wrote,

> Most striking at first is this appearance of sudden illumination, a manifest sign of long, unconscious prior work. The role of this unconscious work in mathematical invention appears to me incontestable, and traces of it would be found in other cases where it is less evident. Often when one works at a hard question, nothing good is accomplished at the first attack. Then one takes a rest, longer or shorter, and sits down anew to the work. During the first half-hour, as before, nothing is found, and then all of a sudden the decisive idea presents itself to the mind. . . . There is another remark to be made about the conditions of this unconscious work: it is possible, and certainly it is only fruitful, if it is on the one hand preceded and on the other hand followed by a period of conscious work. [Hadamard, 1945, p. 38]

This is also emphasized by the poet Amy Lowell:

> How carefully and precisely the subconscious mind functions, I have often been a witness to in my own work. An idea will come into my head for no apparent reason; "The Bronze Horses," for instance. I registered horses as a good subject for a poem; and, having so registered them, I consciously thought no more about the matter. But what I had really done was to drop my subject into the subconscious, much as one drops a letter into the mailbox. Six months later, the words of the poem began to come into my head, the poem—to use my private vocabulary—was "there." [Ghiselin, 1952, p. 110]

Of course creative people are often conscious of some intermediate thoughts in this process. And not all creative work is experienced as spontaneous—some of it is deliberate hard work. This mixture of ingredients goes to make up a completed piece. Listen to Mozart,

> When I am, as it were, completely myself, entirely alone, and of good cheer . . . my ideas flow best and most abundantly. Whence and how they

come, I know not; nor can I force them. Those ideas that please me I retain in memory. . . . If I continue in this way, it soon occurs to me how I may turn this or that morsel to account, so as to make a good dish of it, that is to say, agreeably to the rules of counterpoint, to the peculiarities of the various instruments, etc. [Ghiselin, 1952, p. 44]

No genuine creative work is accomplished in a single conscious-unconscious-conscious leap. Mathematical creation requires a long string of insights and new problem assignments, most of them minor, and only a few dramatic enough to stay in memory. Poincaré may simply have forgotten some intermediate events between the first effortful period of conscious problem-assignment and his memorable "Aha!" experience. Most problem solving requires multiple dives in and out of the stream of consciousness.

Convergence and Divergence

Here is perhaps the single most important feature of the theater image: As Figure 2-1 shows, it combines *convergent input* with *divergent output*. Onto the stage converge the competing actors and their speeches, the makeup artists and scene designers, the playwrights, directors, and acting coaches. Whatever comes to mind reflects a compromise between competition and cooperation, fusing whatever is compatible and excluding for the moment anything that is not. Every dramatic moment, each syllable spoken onstage reflects this convergence of input. Yet as soon as a syllable is pronounced (and this is the aim of the whole enterprise, of course), it floats out to the audience with effects that are largely unknown, but which depend on each individual listener to make of it whatever they will.

Hyppolite Taine, a French historian of the nineteenth century, emphasized these features:

One can compare the mind of a man to a theater of indefinite depth whose apron [i.e., front of the stage] is very narrow but whose stage becomes larger away from the apron. On this lighted apron there is room for one actor only. He enters, gestures for a moment, and leaves; another arrives, then another, and so on. . . . Among the scenery and on the far-off stage . . . unknown evolutions take place incessantly among this crowd of actors of every kind, to furnish the stars who pass before our eyes one by one, as in a magic lantern. [Ellenberger, 1970, p. 270]

Taine suggested that only one actor at a time can come to the footlights, a fact that the nineteenth century called the "narrowness of consciousness," and which we call "limited capacity." It is a very robust finding indeed. "Unknown evolutions take place incessantly" in the far-off, invisible part of the stage, perhaps behind the scenes, "to furnish the stars who pass before our eyes one by one, as in a magic lantern."

A message is broadcast globally, but it is interpreted locally in the mind of each audience member. The director and playwright, listening backstage, are also taking in global messages to guide the next performance. In sum, there is massive convergence of information onto the stage, but once it has come together there, it flows divergently to the audience.

In the next few chapters we will explore the theater metaphor. It is a simple arrangement that we can see working in daily life. This is how classrooms are arranged, and legislative bodies, and scientific conferences. But the metaphor is only a scaffolding, to be discarded without regret once it has outlived its useful days.

Scientific Metaphors

Aren't metaphors pretty crude for thinking about difficult scientific problems? Actually, they have a long and honorable history in science as tools for making the perilous leap from the known to the unknown. The clockwork metaphor of the solar system was of great help to astronomers in the sixteenth century, as a way to think about the swirling interplay among sun, earth, and moon. About 1900 physicists found the Rutherford model of the atom as a tiny solar system useful for generating testable hypotheses. Darwinian evolution was a powerful qualitative metaphor for its first century of existence, and it is often still used so today. Many scientific theories begin in this humble fashion.

Perhaps the best historical example for us is William Harvey's idea in the 1630s that the heart acts as a pump, pushing blood around the body. Harvey's insight challenged a medical tradition going back two thousand years to Galen and Hippocrates. In his time medicine was just beginning to gain an understanding of the body as a great assemblage of cells which all required nutrients, and the notion of the "heart as a pump" cast a great shaft of light into a poorly understood corner of reality. It is a functional metaphor, of course, describing how the heart might serve a certain purpose by propelling the bloodstream through the veins and arteries. Like Harvey's pump metaphor, the theater metaphor describes how conscious and unconscious processes might serve a certain set of functions. There is no literal theater in the brain, any more than the heart has a little windmill carrying tiny scoops of liquid over a dike, as wind-driven pumps moved water in Harvey's seventeenth century. The theater image is just a way to describe the flow of information in the brain.

Scientific metaphors are scaffoldings that help us to grasp and simplify complicated problems. But scaffoldings are useless without real bricks and concrete, and these models are mere doodles on a napkin in the absence of a large constellation of specific research findings: studies of the cellular wiring of the visual cortex, for example, and careful analyses of the remarkable effects of selective brain damage, the role of perception in action control, a century of psychophysical studies, and research on memory, imagery, language, and much more. Those results are indispensible for any unifying theory. Fortunately, we have a wealth of information today that allows us to fill in many gaps. Like any useful framework, the theater metaphor will point to new openings, new questions that can now be asked more clearly.

Like any metaphor, the theater architecture is useful only up to a point; we will keep track of its flaws as well as its uses as we go along. Yet it does provide a useful starting place. In the following chapters we use it to think about a large body of evidence about consciousness. We will not treat the theater metaphor as theory, though all current integrative theories can be thought of as theaters. We will use it just to simplify the evidence.

Limited Capacity and *Vast Access*: Two Views of the Same Mountain

There is an amazing difference in the way psychologists and brain scientists have looked at the brain. Psychologists traditionally see a nervous system that can do only one thing at a time, and which seems to do fairly simple things like mental arithmetic with high rates of errors and a great deal of annoying interference. According to the psychologist, we know only *a single coherent event* in each moment—a visual scene, a mental image, or a fleeting thought. We cannot do two conscious things at a time, such as carrying on an intense conversation and driving in busy traffic. Intermittently conscious tasks can be shared. If we don't need to think much about talking, we can drive at the same time, and vice versa; but the more conscious involvement is needed for each task, the more they will compete against each other. Viewed psychologically, the brain appears to solve simple problems in seconds or even minutes; it makes many errors, tends to sequence even things that might be done at the same time, and its efficiency in solving novel problems is not impressive.

The Vast, Unconscious Brain

From William James to the present, psychologists have thought of consciousness in terms of *selectivity*, a reduction in complexity, while the neuroscientist, looking at the nervous system more directly, finds plentiful evidence for global brain *arousal* but much less for selection. Brain scientists see vast orderly forests of neurons, each receiving input from thousands of others via bushy dendritic twigs and branches, and each with a single output called an *axon*. Neurons send electrical pulses an average of forty times per second through their axons, and they are all active at the same time. The brain is massively parallel, largely unconscious in its details, and widely decentralized in any given task.

At the level of the cells, a structure such as the cerebral cortex is immense—a vast, looming starship unto itself, containing by recent estimates thirty to fifty-five billion neurons. Seen from the outside it is an elaborately folded structure with many rounded hills and folded valleys, neatly tucked into the upper half of the cranial cavity. If we could carefully unfold the great cortical mantle, we would see a sheet about three feet square, with six layers, each composed of myriads of bushy neurons surrounded by supportive cells. This layered sandwich can be parsed into millions of vertical columns and clusters of columns, so that we can imagine a vast six-layered array in three dimensions. Each layer seems to specialize in input, output, or internal connections within the cortex.

Cortical neurons are connected by vast tracts of axonal cables, wrapped in a white sheath called *myelin*. If we simply slice through cortex with a knife, we see mostly white matter, an indication of how many connective cables there are. Seen with the naked eye, cortex looks like a cheesecake covered with a thin layer of cell bodies, the gray matter that we see from the outside. But the white matter contains miles of tiny fibers that descend from the gray cell bodies and end up coming back to cortex. The uppermost layer of the six-layered sandwich, Layer I, is so densely woven horizontally that it has been called a *feltwork*, a large slice of tight webbing on top of the sandwich. While most long-distance communication in cortex seems to run through long, vertical output fibers (axons), the top layer is so tightly interconnected horizontally that many brain scientists believe there is also a great deal of spread within Layer I. Recent evidence suggests that in visual cortex at least, the *innermost* layer of cortex may be the home of conscious sensations.

Cortical neurons project in vast elegant fiber bundles to the neural organs nestled tightly under the cortex, like golf balls beneath a baseball glove. Among the golf balls the thalamus serves as the great traffic hub, the way station for all messages going in and out from cortex, and therefore a strategic control point.

Large pathways project from one hemisphere to the opposite one in mirror-image symmetry, or hang suspended in great fiber bands beneath each hemisphere, connecting frontal and posterior cortex. Current estimates for the corpus callosum—the great fiber bridge that is cut to create split-brain syndrome—are on the order of six hundred million fibers. Each of these fibers send an electrochemical message from forty to almost a thousand times per second, making for message traffic ranging from two hundred to six thousand billion events per second. The whole elegant arrangement obviously limns some regular and mysterious symmetry, if we only knew what it might be.

When we become conscious in the morning, the brain is globally activated, every part showing a sharp spurt in the speed and complexity of neural activity. As novel or surprising events catch our attention, a vast electrical tidal wave rushes all over the brain, three-tenths of a second after the event. Like so many aspects of consciousness in the brain, these facts of consciousness do not look like a reduction but an *increase* in complexity.

Why Is Conscious Capacity So Limited?

Why does consciousness seem so limited in a brain with one hundred billion neurons? This key question is not asked as often as it should be. It isn't just that we have a limited capacity to *do* things—only one mouth to speak with and two hands to fiddle with. The conscious limits are particularly strong in perception, the *input* system, where the limitations of hands and mouth are irrelevant. And it is not that the brain lacks sheer processing capacity—its ability to store and transform information is far beyond our current ability to describe. The narrow limits in psychological tasks come not from in the size or complexity of the brain, but from the fact that we can be conscious of only one unified experience at a time.

If two heads are better than one, why did Mother Nature not find a way to package more than one into a single skull? This is not just a playful question. In the natural world, survival depends on one's ability to drink from a waterhole even while keeping an eye out for predators, all the time making sure that one's offspring don't get lost. It is easy to imagine a host of selective pressures pushing the brain toward an ability to do more than one conscious thing at any given time. But evolution has given us a one-track mind—to be sure, with lots of unconscious things going on at the same time, but only one stream of consciousness. Why?

Here is a possibility. Conscious limits seem to reflect trade-offs in the functioning of the brain. Every evolutionary adaptation involves trade-offs of some kind: adding a huge cortex to our primate brains cost a great deal in allocation of oxygen, glucose, and the like. It is thought that the wide-hipped anatomy of mature women reflects the need for the large head of the infant to pass through the birth canal. The size of the newborn's head makes birth more difficult and painful than it seems to be in other primates. Our sizable cortex carries heavy costs, and presumably there are balancing biological benefits in our ability to plan, to control ourselves, and to think. The following point may be evolution's consolation prize for the narrow limits of consciousness.

Consciousness:
The Gateway to the Unconscious Mind

A few examples give some sense of the global reach of conscious events. We have mentioned the hundred-thousand-word-recognition vocabulary of an educated speaker of English, but that is an underestimate, since most word have multiple meanings, to which we gain access automatically when we hear the word in context.

The size of memory is unknown, but we do know that with recognition tasks we can look at a sequence of up to ten thousand distinct pictures one week, and without attempting to memorize them, simply by *paying attention,* we can recognize this week's pictures and distinguish them from a different set a week later, with more than 95 percent accuracy. That implies that the brain must have stored distinctive information about ten thousand pictures after conscious exposures of perhaps twenty seconds each. It is an awesome accomplishment.

In everyday life we sometimes encounter this large access to memory when we recognize a film seen only once, perhaps many years ago, and can even anticipate the next scene. What about all the melodies you can recognize as familiar? All the faces, the art objects, the artifacts, the people you have known from birth to the present? The fact that we are always conscious of *something,* and that mere conscious-

ness of distinctive events leads to excellent recognition memory, suggests that the amount of information stored is large indeed. Not all of it
can be retrieved at will; but when we make retrieval easy by presenting
the same thing we experienced before, the effects of short conscious
exposures hint at an indefinitely large storage capacity.

Another example of the wide access of consciousness involves
biofeedback training. A few decades ago brain scientists discovered that
humans can control a number of neural functions when they are given
immediate, conscious feedback. For example, the EEG spontaneously
displays a regular alpha-rhythm of eight to twelve cycles per second
some of the time, especially over the visual cortex when the eyes are
closed. It is possible to set up a computer to detect alpha rhythms and
have it emit an audible tone whenever alpha waves occur. The surprise
was how much control this immediate conscious feedback provides
over the alpha rhythm. People soon learn to "go into alpha" at will.

The evidence has now mounted that any single nerve cell, or any population of nerve cells in the brain, can come under voluntary control.
That includes single cells in cortex, in the thalamus and brain stem, and
in the peripheral nerves that pervade the human body. Entire neural
populations can also come under control, such as those in a gigantic
nucleus of the thalamus, in a structure called the *hippocampus,* in parts
of cortex. The alpha-wave activity mentioned above involves millions of
neurons. The power of biofeedback training is an extraordinary finding.
Scientists perhaps take it too much for granted. The implications are
significant because it suggests that all neurons in the brain can become
involved with the conscious, voluntary, limited-capacity system: the part
of us that controls most of our actions.

It is not emphasized often enough that biofeedback training always
requires *conscious* feedback. To gain control over alpha waves in the
EEG we pay attention to a tone or light corresponding to the increased
alpha activity; to gain control over single cortical neurons we play back
a conscious click for each peak of electrical activity, and so on. Under
such conditions, people can learn to control an extremely wide range of
physiological activities with surprising ease. A small needle electrode
in the base of the thumb can record the activity of a single motor
"unit"—just one muscle fiber controlled by a motor neuron coming
from the spinal cord and a sensory one going back to it. When a single
neuron fires and the electrical event is amplified and played through a
loudspeaker, it sounds like a sharp click. A subject can learn to control
the click in about ten minutes, so that it occurs at will, and some have
been able to play drumrolls on their single motor unit after thirty min-

utes of practice! Whatever interferes with conscious feedback impedes biofeedback learning.

If we keep in mind the fact that you and I have no idea how we control our muscles, a complex and subtle process that is not available to consciousness, the question arises, Who or what is doing the learning in biofeedback? Common sense says that "we" are learning, as if there is some centralized self that is in control of all the details. But that cannot be true, because the everyday "we" has no access to the necessary information. If we think of the brain as a massive decentralized society of biocomputers, it may be more realistic to say that the motor system is learning something, *based on conscious information that is made available to many unconscious local control systems.* We are not doing the learning; they are.

We can draw an analogy between biofeedback training and finding a lost child in a large city. At first we search *locally,* around home or school. But if the child cannot be found there, it makes sense to broadcast a global message to all the people in the city: "Have you seen Jerry or Martha?" Only those who have relevant information need to answer back. The message is global, but only local experts feed back their information. This is what we would expect if conscious feedback were made available throughout the brain, and local processors decided whether to respond to it.

This is of course the message of the theater metaphor. It is what we mean when we say that consciousness seems to create *vast access* to perhaps all parts of the nervous system.

Although it seems that any neural system can potentially come under voluntary control, it would be absurd to try to control heart rate or the movements of the intestines, because doing so would load working memory capacity with all its limitations; and consciously we lack the wisdom needed to run the heart, for example, as well as the body does unconsciously. Most of the business of body and brain is conducted with great skill by unconscious processes without moment-to-moment conscious control. Consider how may ordinary actions are run by automatic components of action: talking, listening, viewing a scene, reacting emotionally, interpreting a social situation, relating to others, playing chess, driving a car, walking, loving, dancing, teasing, arguing, making peace after an argument. Automatisms can be evoked by a distinctive stimulus, such as the reading habits that fire quickly when you see any *known word,* the gestures of a friend, a familiar face from ten years ago, a signal of instinctive danger. Even years after we have learned to swim, if we are accidentally thrown into water, we can recapture in seconds the automatic components of swimming.

Learning as a Magical Process

The idea that consciousness is a gateway, something that creates access to a vast unconscious mind, has interesting implications for our understanding of learning. It suggests that *the real work of learning is simply to point one's consciousness to some information to be learned,* allowing the detailed processes of learning to take place unconsciously. It is as if learning occurs magically, without effort or deliberate guidance, carried out by a skilled squad of unconscious helpers.

For twenty years cognitive scientists have tried to encode the knowledge human experts have about physics, computer programming, and medicine in large computerized semantic networks. The big lesson of those years is that expert knowledge is highly *domain specific,* that is, that medical knowledge, for example, is so different from physics that almost nothing in one area applies to the other. And yet as human beings we do pretty much one thing with anything we need to learn: we merely bring it to consciousness, and learning somehow occurs. It looks like sheer magic.

The radical simplicity of learning is quite extraordinary. We direct our attention to the formula $x = y + 3$, play with its elements and rules, and somehow, with no *detailed* conscious coding of the information, we acquire the ability to grasp it as a whole with a genuine sense of understanding. We learn to see new visual patterns simply by paying attention to a set of X-rays or a series of Flemish still-life paintings. We learn to hear in new ways merely by listening to birdsongs or symphonies. The regularities of language are acquired simply by paying attention to the sentences we hear.

Yet we know that language activates an utterly different part of the brain than visual events do, which are yet again different from planning and feeling, fine motor control, learning what foods taste good, and hundreds of other specialized aspects of conscious information. Paying attention—becoming conscious of some material—seems to be the sovereign remedy for learning all these very different kinds of information. Consciousness is the universal solvent of the mind.

From this point of view, the *content* of learning is usually unconscious. Children learning language don't consciously label the words they hear as nouns or verbs. Rather, they pay attention to speech sounds, and the underlying grammar is learned *implicitly.* We rarely become conscious of abstract patterns—the regularities of grammar, the harmonic progressions of a symphony, or the delicate brushwork of Vermeer. Most knowledge is tacit knowledge; most learning is implicit.

Did Evolution Discover Theaters First?

Theaters are useful. Their fundamental features are found in classrooms, scientific conferences, television sets, broadcasting, armies, bureaucracies, and business organizations. It may be that evolutionary biology discovered the same style of functioning eons ago. Quite different animals may solve similar problems in similar ways, and human technology occasionally rediscovers biological solutions as well. Computers were invented a billion years after nervous systems, but they have important similarities. The Romans invented the arch ages after evolution discovered the rib, but the principle of strength through arched construction is the same. At twilight, darting swallows in pursuit of insects zig and zag rapidly by tilting ninety degrees to the horizon whenever they change direction; jet fighters needing to turn fast do the same because they follow the same laws of aerodynamics. Homologies like this are the rule, not the exception, and the theater architecture may be just another example.

We have now sketched one way of thinking about our experience. Over the next few chapters we will see how far it will take us. What can we make of the stage, the spotlight, the audience and those mysterious goings-on behind the scenes?

Further Reading

Allan Newell and Herbert A. Simon's *Human Problem Solving* (1972) is still the best source on the first twenty years of cognitive modeling by means of theater models. More recent works along these lines include Newell's last book, *Unified Theories of Cognition* (1990). John R. Anderson has written several books tracing the development of his unified theory, notably *The Architecture of Cognition* (1983). One of the nicest informal presentations of a theater model is in Peter Lindsay and Donald A. Norman's *Human Information Processing* (1977). The history of the unconscious is thoroughly covered in Henri Ellenberger's classic *Discovery of the Unconscious* (1970).

« **t h r e e** »

ONSTAGE:
SENSATIONS, IMAGES, AND IDEAS

Philosophers have long divided conscious events into sensations, which have perceptual qualities like color and shape, and abstract ideas, which do not. If you can imagine this morning's breakfast, you can probably visualize the eggs, the toast, and the orange juice. But visualizing the abstract concept of "daily nutrition" is much harder. The world of sensation is unparalleled in richness and precision along all the qualitative dimensions of color, texture, taste, and touch. As Aristotle observed, mental images are like faint copies of sensations, so that vision seems to be mimicked by visual imagery, and inner speech echoes physical speech. We now know that Aristotle was right: there is a close overlap between the brain areas involved in perception and imagery. Images and inner speech are truly internally created sensations.

However, ideas seem to be different. Like the abstract concept of "nutrition" compared to your mental image of this morning's breakfast, ideas seem to lack sensory qualities; they have no color, no texture, and no fine-grained detail. Yet they resemble sensory experiences in other ways. Conscious ideas occur one after another (serially), they are highly structured and internally consistent, and they compete for access to consciousness. For example, it is hard to look at a beautiful painting and think about a difficult conceptual problem at the same time.

Even if we cannot appreciate sensations and concepts at the very same instant, most of the time we are dealing with both almost at the same time. This printed sentence, for example, has visual qualities, and if you are using inner speech as you read this, it evokes some auditory ones as well. But it also has meaning. When sensory and conceptual levels are consistent with each other, they may coexist in consciousness, perhaps not in the same instant but at least over a period of seconds and longer. The most moving poetry, the most enduring encounters with others, join the abstract and concrete levels of experience.

Consciousness Has a Sensory Bias

Sensory perception has distinctive and robust qualities, what philosophers call *qualia*: colors, textures, the taste of salt, sour, and sweet, smooth and rough touch, wetness, sharp and dull pain, focused and vague pleasures, the dull variety of stomachaches, jolts of fear and blazing anger, itches and muscle pains, melodies and rhythms, the acrid odor of gunpowder, musical harmony and dissonance, the crack and rumble of a thunderstorm. Nothing by comparison is as rich and full of nuance, or as compelling in presence and urgency.

The sense modalities include the five classic senses plus many submodalities like heat, pain, and pleasure. Conscious percepts leave a fast-fading trace in our minds that can be measured. Children on a camping trip often discover how you can take a stick with a glowing ember from the campfire, and rotate it against the night sky to show a sparkling trail. If you swing the glowing stick in a circle about two feet across until it forms a visible circle, the circumference of the circle gives a good approximation for the decay time of visual sensation, a few seconds long. Methods like this agree roughly on the time of the fleeting visual present, and similar durations have been found for the conscious sensory echo of sound and touch. Similar methods can be used to establish the duration of the auditory and tactile trace. The chemical senses—smell and taste—last as long as stimulating molecules are present at the receptor surfaces in our nose and mouth, until the senses adapt to them, perhaps ten seconds or a little longer.

All the qualities of the outer senses seem to be echoed in the inner senses, evoked by purely internal sources. Visual *images* resemble real visual sensations, and *inner speech* has much in common with overt speech.

It is interesting to compare the clarity and detail of consciousness in sensory input, to output processes of speech and action, and intervening mental processes like thinking. Sensory perception *is* the input mode of the nervous system, and we are exquisitely conscious of the details of each sense impression. But *thinking* seems to be devoid of conscious qualities, except where it involves inner speech; but inner speech seems to be a simulation of ordinary outer speech input. Likewise, if we look at speech and action we seem to have much less conscious appreciation of details than in sensation, except where actions create sensory feedback, which is of course nothing but sensory input again!

In sum, it seems as if we get our most detailed conscious information from sensations, or simulated inner sensations: qualitative, percept-like events. Try raising your eyebrows, for example. Did you know which muscles to contract? Now compare this knowledge to *seeing yourself* raising your eyebrows in a mirror. Which task provides more detailed information, *doing it* or *seeing yourself doing it*? It is commonly reported that we have little or no conscious access to the details in action control, while perception is full of rich detail.

Perception of the physical world may be the most ancient mode of consciousness. The sensory systems are evolutionarily old and very highly developed. Sensory perception is necessary for survival in a world that arose long before cultural evolution began to explode with challenges to our Paleolithic brains, only ten thousand years ago. Before that time humans were hunter-gatherers in a relatively stable environment over millions of years, and it is in that Stone Age environment that our brains developed from the primate stock.

What differentiates humans from other primates is the growth of cortex, but not sensory cortex. Vision, audition, touch and taste, and especially smell, are well developed in all primates, and indeed in most mammals. Humans have some additional patches of specialized cortex to handle speech perception, facial recognition, and the like. But the greatest amount of new cortex, as shown by our bulging foreheads, is not sensory or even linguistic; it is the part that involves abstraction, planning, and the control of self in action.

A Dip Into the Wet Brain: Vision

More is known about vision than about any other sense modality. Figure 3-1 shows the location of the primary visual cortex at the rear tip of the brain. and a horizontal slice in cross section. The optic tract begins at each eye, stops off at the thalamus, and terminates in the

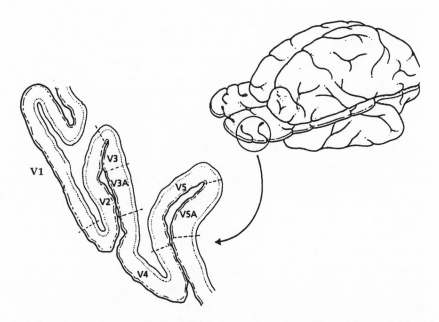

Figure 3-1. *Some of the sites of conscious experience.* The early visual projection areas are shown in this horizontal slice of visual cortex, taken from the rear of the brain. Visual information flows from the eyes to the thalamus, then to V1 and up, ultimately to perhaps forty separate areas for visual analysis. The first five visual areas, V1 to V5, shown here, are believed to be deeply involved in visual consciousness. Damage to the first visual area, V1, leads to *blindsight*, in which there is still some visual knowledge, but patients strongly deny having visual *consciousness*.

first part of visual cortex, called V1. Like all cortex, the visual region is a deeply folded sheet. If the early visual areas V1 to V5 were unfolded, they would show five increasingly integrative maps of the retina; any two neighboring points on the retina are also next to each other in V1-V5.

Area V1, the first place where information from the eyes reaches the cortex, responds to a few basic properties of the visual, input a little bit like a black-and-white television screen that represents only dots of light. The nerve cells in V1 are sensitive to light points surrounded by darker contrast, and dark points surrounded by lighter contrast; to short straight bars of light and dark, at many different orientations; and to moving bars of light. Each of the other visual areas from V2 to V5 detects its own particular visual features, and most feed back to preceding areas. V2 appears to specialize in orientation and color; V3 seems to deal with shape; V4 is largely devoted to color; and V5 is specialized in motion detection.

From this early analysis, visual information goes on to higher areas, up to what are now believed to be over forty different visual analyzers, including patches of tissue specialized in deciphering objects, faces, location, and the like. Starting from areas V4 and V5, the visual brain begins to transmit information to the frontal cortex and other parts of the brain. In theater terms, this is the point where the visual actors begin to speak to their audience.

But we do not see the world only in points of light; we see objects, faces, textures, shapes, complex motions, and entire visual events. Those higher-level aspects are an essential part of our visual experience. As Francis Crick and Christof Koch point out, they are not explicitly represented in early visual cortex at all (1990). Cells that represent these higher-level clumps of visual meaning are found along the bottom of the temporal cortex and the top of parietal cortex, covering, in a broad sense, the entire rear half of the visible brain. In that sense, our conscious experience of the sensory world cannot be reduced to a few areas: it results from the rear half of the entire cortical mantle, some twenty billion neurons, perhaps.

Yet there is something special about early visual cortex. That special contribution is brought out most clearly in a remarkable type of brain damage called *blindsight,* perhaps the single most revealing key to the great puzzle of perceptual consciousness. Semir Zeki, one of the foremost researchers on visual cortex, even speaks of "experiential neurons" in this part of the brain. Here is the reason why.

Blindsight: A Deep Puzzle

Only one kind of brain damage seems to selectively abolish visual consciousness itself. Some stroke patients sustain damage to area V1, just where the optic radiations first reach the cortex. Scientists Ernst Pöppel and Larry Weiskrantz were among the first to study this remarkable deficit. Blindsight patients get visual information from the world just as the rest of us do, but *they say they are not visually conscious of it.* If you show them a cup of coffee they claim not to see it; yet forced to guess, they are surprisingly accurate. They can reach for the visual object quite accurately, point to its location, detect large differences in pattern and even color, and track it with their eyes. Yet they vehemently insist they have no visual experience of the coffee cup.

We must not overlook the human tragedy of blindsight, but from these disasters in the lives of people we learn that visual consciousness is something more than just knowledge. To have the experience of *visual* consciousness, that rich array of color and detail, of shading, reflections of the light, textures, objects and events, we need area V1. And we now have similar reports from analogous damage in the other sensory systems. Neuropsychologists have found patients suffering from "deaf hearing" after damage to the first auditory area (A1) and of "blind touch" from damage to the first somatosensory area (S1). These disorders are also marked by "knowing" without sensory consciousness. In spite of disagreements over details, there is now a good consensus that blindsight and its analogues provide us with a key feature of one kind of conscious experience.

The mystery of blindsight is not so much that unconscious visual knowledge remains. Larry Weiskrantz has pointed out that at least ten "minor" pathways have been found, going from the eyes to the cortex, in addition to the great highway of the visual tract that normally leads to conscious vision. The greatest puzzle seems to be that information that is not even represented in area V1 is lost to consciousness when V1 is damaged. Let's state that in another way: V1 is the only region whose loss abolishes our ability to consciously see objects, events, people, dramatic gestures, delicate textures, the bold shapes of a Picasso painting. But the cells in V1 respond only to a sort of pointillist level of visual perception, like the dots of light on a television screen. Thus it seems that area V1 is needed for such higher-level experiences, even though it does not contain higher-level elements! It seems like a paradox.

Cells that recognize objects, shapes, and textures appear only in much "higher" regions of cortex, strung in a series of specialized regions along the bottom of the temporal lobe. Here we find the areas that support our visual knowledge of objects and faces, for example. Damage to these areas results in failures of object perception called *visual agnosia:* a patient might be able to read small print, but cannot visually recognize a wristwatch. Holding the watch by hand allows recognition by touch, so that we know the deficit is in the visual system. And the ability to read small print indicates that conscious visual resolution is intact, quite different from blindsight. Some scientists argue that visual agnosia is also a deficit of consiousness, as indeed it is. But damage to V1 "blocks out" *all* higher-level visual consciousness, while damage to object perception causes only a local loss. Thus the effects are quite different from each other.

Perhaps the greatest puzzle we face today is this: how are we to think about the relationship between V1 and the higher visual areas? Where does consciousness reside?

Here is the evidence in a little more detail.

The Locus of Visual Experience?

The brain is an immensely complex and often surprising organ; brain scientists commonly devote entire careers to even small territories within that great continent. Even stating reasonable hypotheses about brain functions can be very tricky indeed.

For that reason, it is important to look for several convergent lines of evidence to support any viable hypothesis. In addition to blindsight, which implicates area V1 in visual consciousness, there is further support for the involvement of early parts of visual cortex in visual consciousness. The evidence comes from

1. *Direct stimulation.* It has been known for many years that a low-current electrode applied to the sensory cortex in vision, hearing, and the body senses will evoke corresponding conscious sensations. This is not true in other parts of cortex.

2. *Recording from single nerve cells.* Nikos Logothetis and Jeffrey Schall have now found remarkable experimental verification that the visual brain in monkeys behaves exactly the way the human brain does, when it is confronted with binocular rivalry: It will create coherence even in the face of competing visual inputs. Logothetis and Schall (1989) used motion rivalry between two visual streams, a grating moving upward in front of one eye and downward in front of the other, like two opposite escalators. Since the two streams of information seem to be in the same spatial location, they cannot be interpreted as two separate streams, and one of the two is always suppressed. To humans it looks as if the visual escalator goes up one moment and down the next. Question: Will the same phenomenon occur in macaque monkeys, with visual brains much like our own? Or, to put it more boldly, do macaques have coherent visual consciousness, as we do?

Logothetis and Schall trained monkeys to indicate whether they saw the visual escalators going up or down, which is easy to do simply by presenting *one* visual flow at a time. Not surprisingly, macaques easily learned to signal when they perceived an up or down-flowing grating, with perfect accuracy. Then the two opposing streams were presented simultaneously, one to each eye. Macaques chose one *or* the other, exactly the way humans do, occasionally changing between the two interpretations. To explore the brain location of the effect, the scientists recorded the activity of single neurons in the part of visual cortex that responds to motion (called area *V5*, or *MT*) and found, indeed, that more motion-sensitive neurons fired in the direction that the monkeys indicated they were perceiving.

It seems that Logothetis and Schall accomplished a historic feat in finding the brain correlates of a conscious visual experience. Obviously the experience of a visual grating flowing up or down involves many brain neurons, but the *direction of motion* is the essential difference. It is what makes it possible to respond "up" or "down" for humans, and for monkeys to indicate the same thing with a lever.

This study is a prototype of excellent consciousness research. It is carefully designed to treat consciousness as a variable, using a visual effect that is clear and powerful in humans, and is therefore likely to have major brain correlates in primates with similar visual systems. Cortical recording of ambiguous information is becoming increasingly possible with the growth of neuroimaging techniques, and we are likely to see further studies following on this landmark work.

3. *Brain imaging of visual consciousness.* This is perhaps the most promising. The evidence from brain imaging studies can be seen in Insert 2 in the color section. As you can see, early visual cortex "lights up" in the computer-generated maps of the brain based on PET scans. "Lit up" areas represents increased consumption of oxygen and glucose, needed to feed neurons that are working harder than others in the scan. What is important for us is that the early visual projection areas, which we believe include conscious vision, light up when people tell us that they are indeed conscious of the visual stimulus. Likewise Insert 3 in the color section shows auditory cortex lighting up when people report a conscious sound.

The Wet Wiring Is only the Beginning of the Story

We now have a very rough description of the early visual wiring diagram, but that is not nearly enough: the real question is how neural activity flows along those "wires," and here we must make note of the fact that in cortex essentially *all connections go in both directions*, "upward" and "downward" (see Figure 3.2). Information flows from the visual relay station of the thalamus to cortical area V1, and back again; from V1 to V2, and the other way; and so on. In fact, we know that really stable neural traces (for time periods of seconds to perhaps minutes) seem to involve two-way reentrant loops. Gerald Edelman has made the case that all conscious events seem to require such loops,

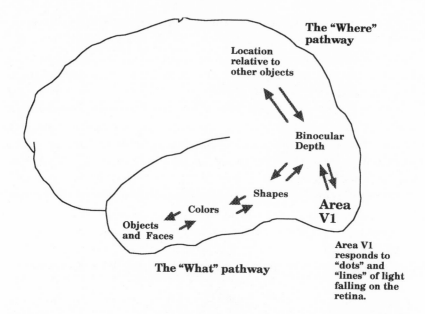

The "Where" pathway

Location relative to other objects

Binocular Depth

Shapes

Colors

Area V1

Objects and Faces

The "What" pathway

Area V1 responds to "dots" and "lines" of light falling on the retina.

Figure 3-2. *The "what" and "where" pathways in the visual brain.* We are visually conscious of points and lines of light and dark, of colors, textures, shapes, and movements—all at the same time. Yet these aspects of visual consciousness are recognized at separate locations in the brain; shapes, colors, and objects along the bottom of the temporal cortex, locations along the top of the parietal lobe. How does the brain "bind" these separate analyzers into a single conscious experience? Francis Crick and Rodolfo Llinás have proposed a *temporal* binding mechanism. There may be *spatial* binding as well to tie each visual feature to a particular point in the visual field. Area V1 may act as a "retinotopic coordinating map," organizing many visual features into a single conscious whole. (Figure adapted from Posner and Raichle, 1994, p. 15.)

and similar arguments emerge from neural net modeling techniques.

Visual consciousness would seem to involve a series of interlocking activation loops. One cycles between thalamus and V1; a second, complex set of interacting loops flows among the early visual areas V1 to V5. A further set of loops seems to go to higher visual areas representing objects, facial features, and the like, in different parts of the temporal cortex; and location of the visual object is coded along the top of the brain well into the parietal cortex. The whole Ferris wheel of active loops is probably modulated by the executive attentional network discussed in the next few chapters.

A Solution to the Puzzle of Blindsight?
Area V1 as a Spatial Coordinating Map

The fundamental question is how V1 could be so important to visual consciousness, when the higher areas are needed to represent objects and other higher-order visual units. One reasonable hypothesis is that the major function of V1 may be to *coordinate* all the visual areas in a single spatial coordinate system. It is as if we have a small orchestra, playing parts from the same musical sore. Each instrument could do its job perfectly, and yet, if all were not playing together, the result would be noise. A conductor is needed to *pace* all of the instruments, so that they play in unison. Area V1 may be such a coordinator, not in time but in retinotopic space. To draw the analogy, we know that up to forty separate regions of the rear half of the brain must be coordinated, so that the points represented in V1 correspond to colored points in V2 and V4, as elements of a moving object in V5, as a part of a coffee cup in yet higher levels. Spatial coordination must be maintained to keep all these areas "lined up," identified as the same location in retinal space. On a color television screen, that job is accomplished by a raster, a large grid coded in a chip, so that the red, blue, and green electron guns are aimed precisely at the right point on the screen, their colors mixing together to come up with just one single glowing pixel of aquamarine. In the brain, if the forty areas of visual representation are not locked into a single retinotopic map, their activities might not fuse to form a single visual scene. The result might never add up to a coherent display in consciousness.

In the technical jargon, V1 may be needed for spatial "binding," tying many visual areas into a single retinotopic display. A similar argument, discussed in the following section, has been made for temporal binding by Rodolfo Llinás and Francis Crick.

But Waking Consciousness Is Necessary
to See Anything

As we have seen in Chapter 1, the state of waking consciousness is mediated by two small parts of the central core of the brain, the reticular formation and the intralaminar nuclei of the thalamus. When these areas are damaged, people fall into coma. Waking consciousness is a necessary condition for visual consciousness—so what is the relationship between the waking state and the cortical contents of consciousness?

We could suppose that the intralaminar nuclei (ILN) correspond to the stage of the conscious theater, but that is unlikely. They may be too small to carry all the richness of a visual scene, for example. Francis Crick has suggested that a related thalamic nucleus, called the *reticular nucleus* (nRt), may control the gates of the major thalamic nuclei that send their information to the sensory areas of cortex. The reticular nucleus is known to be involved in *selection* of one pathway or another to sensory cortex. It could well be the traffic cop, but not the traffic. It is not itself a source of conscious experience.

One of the basic questions raised in recent years by Francis Crick, among others, is this: How do all the different neurons in the visual cortex combine their specific information into a single, coherent conscious experience? How is temporal binding achieved? One possibility is a pacing rhythm, a widespread, oscillating electrical signal that could entrain many different neurons to dance in rhythm with each other.

The most attractive candidate for such a pacing rhythm is a forty-times-per-second oscillation proposed by Rodolfo Llinás and Crick. Llinás in particular has developed much evidence on behalf of what has come to be known as "the forty-Hertz hypothesis" (Llinás and Ribary, 1992). The reticular nucleus nRt and ILN are believed to be active sources of forty-hertz oscillations, in Llinás's account sweeping from the front of the cortex to the back of the brain at regular intervals.

In sum, the early parts of visual cortex, including Area V1 may be essential to visual conscious experience, by acting as a cpatial coordinator, holding all the active higher visual areas in a single retinal coordinate system.

The thalamic nuclei responsible for the *state* of waking consciousness may provide the forty-Hertz signal to pace what Semir Zeki has called "the experiential neurons" in visual cortex together with thalamic areas needed to maintain the state of consciousness.

Lastly, the selective attention system in the thalamus may open the visual gates in coordination with ILN, so that information from the eyes flows to cortex at the same time that a 40 Hertz pacing rhythm works to coordinate all the visual areas in cortex.

This seems to be a reasonable story today, but we do not know nearly enough yet to tell if is really true.

The Consciousness Network:
Does the Theater Have Five Stages?

Are the basic sensory contents of consciousness represented in all the early projection areas? Is it possible that the early visual areas correspond to the stage of the visual theater, that early auditory areas constitute the sound stage, and early somatosensory areas may be the feeling stage? Instead of having one stage in our theater of consciousness, we may have five, switching rapidly back and forth several times per second. We can then suggest a *sensory consciousness network* to provide the basis for qualitative conscious experience.

As we will see, a sensory consciousness network may provide the foundation for the inner conscious senses as well as the outer ones, and even for abstract, conscious ideas.

Imagery and Self-Talk: The Inner Theater

There is now solid evidence that imagery and perception differ primarily in the source of information: In perception the source is the outer senses, while in imagery it is the brain itself.

Can you imagine an elephant? See if you can view it from the side, from head to tail, the great flank, the ears, the small curling tail. Now walk around to its front—don't get too close—where you can see it head-on, from a distance of about twenty paces. Stand in front of the elephant so that you can see both eyes and now imagine a fly crawling over its left eyelid. Did you just zoom in on the elephant's eyelid to see the fly? Everyone I've asked this question reports having done so. What about your image of the elephant, when you zoom in? When we move close to a small object with the physical eye, the rest of the scene overflows the visual field. As we zoom out again, the larger image comes back into focus. But why does imagery resemble the vision so closely? Do we have a visual field in our heads?

Cognitive scientist Stephen Kosslyn has demonstrated that "the mind's eye" is a surprisingly realistic figure of speech (1980). The human visual field has a characteristic size and shape, which is easy to show. Simply look at the room in which you are reading this, allowing your eyes to move, but without moving your head. Now bring your hands in from the sides of your visual field until you can barely see them; the horizontal limits of the active visual field will be on the order of 120 degrees of visual arc. Do the same for the vertical limits, and it will turn out to be less than half of that. The *working* visual field seems to be a flat oval, let's say 45 degrees in height by 120 degrees wide. This estimate depends critically on allowing the eyes to move normally, without moving your head and without forcing the eyes far into the corners of the field.

You can measure your inner field of imagery exactly the way you did your visual field, by using your imaginary hands (of course!). Closing your eyes, move your virtual hands to the sides of the imagery

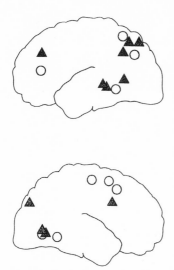

Figure 3-3. *The similarity between visual perception and visual mental images.* These brain diagrams (left hemisphere above and right hemisphere below) show areas that are active during visual imagery, in which people are asked to imagine a visual event (triangles), and a closely matched visual perception task in which people actually see the event (circles). The high degree of overlap between the two suggests that visual imagery makes use of the same parts of cortex that evolved to represent the visual world. (Reprinted with permission from Kosslyn, S. M. Aspects of a Cognitive Neuroscience of Mental Imagery. *Science*, 240. Copyright © 1988 American Association for the Advancement of Science.)

domain, and write down the horizontal extent of your field. Now do the same in the vertical dimension. People generally will come up with somewhat less than 120 degrees of horizontal arc, and about 45 degrees vertical.

A variety of such experiments show a remarkable resemblance between the physical visual field and its mental double. Over the last several years research has begun to reveal the reason for this remarkable resemblance. Stephen Kosslyn and Martha Farah have shown extensively that visual imagery elicits activity in the same parts of cortex as visual perception (Kosslyn, 1988). In other words, in generating mental images in the mind's eye, we use the same piece of brain that interprets the physical eye (see Figure 3-3).

It is, in a way, a confirmation of a long-standing hypothesis. In the sixth century B.C. Aristotle, an extraordinary scientific observer, suggested that images are "faint copies of sensations." I suppose this must be a record for length of time between prediction and verification of a psychological hypothesis, about twenty-five hundred years.

Could it be that perception—and imagery, which rides on it—is the only conscious modality that has qualities? Is it the only one we ever experience in detail? I think it is quite possible. Abstract concepts have no mental qualities such as color and warmth. But before exploring our experience of abstractions, consider first the foremost mental tool we have for thinking abstractly: the tool of language.

That Little Inner Voice

Consider for a moment the little voice in the back of your head. (If it just said, "what little voice?"—that's the one!) Most of us go around the world talking to ourselves. Just by noticing it more, we can come to realize how often we talk to ourselves in the privacy of our minds, sometimes addressing a completely imaginary jury—of professional peers, family, or you, the reader—in a sort of simulated reality. People are often quite willing to tell us about their private monologue. Simply by asking them to write down clear internal speech as soon as it occurs, a body of useful evidence has been gathered.

We are a gabby species. The urge to talk to ourselves is remarkably compelling, as we can easily see by trying to *stop* the inner voice as long as possible. My limit for self-imposed inner silence seems to be about five seconds, and while people no doubt differ to some extent, no one I have asked reports silences that go much longer. As an experiment it is quite interesting to try it a few times, just to see how predictable the urge to talk really is; or ask a few friends to try it just to see how long they can keep inner silence. Inner speech is one of the basic facts of human nature, one that takes only a minute to demonstrate. It seems to be utterly basic to the human condition. Most of us seem to spend far more hours per day talking to ourselves than to other people.

If we include *inner speech* in the inner senses, we can even find similarities between inner and outer articulation of words. Insert 4 in the color section presents a remarkable PET scan taken during quiet mental rehearsal—an aspect of Working Memory. It shows bright spots (areas of high brain activity) in the two parts of the brain known to be involved in speech input and output. The forward bright spot includes Broca's area, the part of cortex that controls vocal output. The posterior one centers around Wernicke's area, needed for hearing and understanding speech. These areas are named after nineteenth-century neurologists who first studied patients with devastating local damage to these parts of the brain. Broca's patient was unable to speak but could hear and understand speech; Wernicke's patient suffered from a receptive deficit alone. Just as in visual imagery, Insert 4 shows that the parts of the brain responsible for external speech are also at work in inner speech. The inner senses imitate the outer senses.

We must not make the mistake of interpreting every bright spot in a brain image as conscious. Consider the hot spot in Broca's area, which controls speech output, the extraordinarily subtle, rapid and delicate activity of the speaking muscles. More than a hundred muscle groups are known to be invovled in speaking, timing their actions with millisecond precision. In saying the syllable /pa/ we must open our lips twenty milliseconds before starting to sound the vowel. That time interval is critical: Without it, the sound is heard as /ba/. Are we conscious of this delicate difference in muscle control? Of course not.

As we noted in the beginning of this chapter, consciousness seems to have a sensory bias: There are strong arguments for the idea that we are far more conscious of *input* than *output*. Perceptually we can clearly tell the difference between the sound of /pa/ and /ba/, but we have no idea how to instruct our vocal muscles to carry out that twenty-millisecond time lag. One could imagine a nervous system in which detailed action commands would be consciously available, but that is not how the human brain works. A great body of evidence show that we control actions by means of perceptual feedback, an input process. We listen to ourselves in order to speak. If this is true, of the two hot spots in Insert 4, only Wernicke's area is conscious.

Yet internal speech seems to involve a definite output component. The psycholinguist Gary Dell has shown that internal tongue twisters create errors very similar to overt tongue twisters. Try repeating "Peter piper picked a peck of pickled peppers" in your inner speech, for example. Do you notice inner pronunciation errors? But you have no real inner tongue to twist, or do you? Inner practice seems to aid outer performance. Artists and musicians often describe such imagery skills, and athletes find it helps to mentally practice pole vaulting or golf shots to improve their performance. Imaginary practice can be very effective—which makes a lot of sense if we use the same bits of brain tissue for mental and physical practice.

Mental images play a horrific role in phobias, post-traumatic stress, and schizophrenia. Phobia can be considered a disorder of imagery control: even with no realistic danger of falling from a high building, phobics still play catastrophic images to themselves, paralyzed with fear just as if their images were real. Some therapy techniques are aimed to change the mental images that phobic individuals struggle against so valiantly, and they have a good success rate. In one technique, called "practicing the symptom," phobia victims are taught to deliberately manipulate their images of the feared event: to approach the edge of a tall building in their imagination, look over the edge, and even jump. Since you can do anything in your imagination, you can also imagine flying, or leaping back onto the parapet, or hitting the ground perfectly intact like a character in a cartoon. The point of the exercise is to give people a sense of their own ability to shape and select their mental images, rather than feel trapped in the seeming inevitability of the phobic catastrophe. Learning to play with a catastrophic image often leads to relief from phobia.

Schizophrenic hallucinations are often extremely upsetting and may also involve inner sensations that have run out of control. Auditory hallucinations are the most common. Many people who suffer from these syndromes live in dread of some sadistic voice of doom shouting horrible accusations in their minds, knowing their inmost thoughts, seeming completely out of control. Yet almost all humans talk to themselves. Can you whisper in your inner speech? Shout? Put on a monster voice? A child's voice? Such schizophrenic hallucinations may come from inner speech that has run out of control. I do not know of any treatment that aims to teach schizophrenics to speak to themselves in different voices, at will, to regain control over the inner voice. Perhaps they can learn eventually to turn down the volume on auditory hallucinations. It would seem to be worth trying.

Images Are Concrete and Individual

Take a look around you: The world of perceptual experience is populated by concrete exemplars of things, books, tables and chairs, windows, people. You have never seen an abstract class of chairs or heard a general phenomenon. The sense modalities provide us not with general knowledge but with particulars, and mental imagery, which mimics sensation and perception, does the same.

In philosophy, where intellectual wars are long and passionate, Plato raised another mare's nest 2,500 years ago: the problem of abstract ideas versus concrete perceptions. Consciousness of ideas, he noticed, seems to apply to classes of events, but sensory consciousness always refers to particulars. I suspect in the beginning this philosophical battle was about mental images, for the word "idea" in Greek (ideon) means "image". The question is how does one mentally represent an abstract class of objects, such as the class of automobiles or the class of quadratic equations? George Berkeley pointed out in 1710 that he, at least, could imagine no abstract images.

> Whether others have this wonderful faculty of abstracting their ideas [images] they best can tell. For myself, I find I have indeed a faculty of imagining, or representing to myself, the idea of those particular things I have perceived, and of variously compounding and dividing them. I can imagine a man with two heads, or the upper parts of a man joined

to the body of a horse. I can consider the hand, the eye, the nose, each by itself abstracted or separated from some particular shape and colour. Likewise the idea of man that I frame to myself must be either of a white, or a black, or a tawny, a straight, or a crooked, a tall, or a low, or a middle-sized man. I cannot by any effort of thought conceive the abstract idea. [p. 7]

And yet, the concept of "consciousness," which we have referred to a few times in this book, is pretty abstract. What have you and I been doing in the last few chapters when we thought we were conscious of the meaning of all these ideas about consciousness?

Are Ideas Conscious?

Language psychologists have known for decades that people convert the sentences they hear into an abstract code within a second or two, while losing the specific words heard. This is easy to prove on the spot, with a little demonstration that may test the tolerance of your friends. In the middle of a conversation, ask them, *"What did I just say?"* Almost no one will be able to repeat your actual words, but they will be able to *paraphrase* what you just said if they were paying attention at all. But what is a paraphrase? It is a different sentence, with different words, different grammar, and a different speaker in a different vocal style, *but it preserves meaning.* When meaning is the only thing preserved, it follows that it must have been the only thing retained for recall. This spontaneous paraphrase effect works quickly, only a second or two after a listener hears a sentence, indicating that we recode a heard sentence quite rapidly.

There are many ways to do this little experiment; for example, you could do it in the middle of this page by closing the book at some arbitrary moment and asking yourself, *"What did I just read?"* You'll see the same thing: Meaning tends to be preserved, while words, grammar, and the "outer form" of the sentence is lost.

Semantic coding is a very useful human strategy for taking in information because the meaning level packs in more useful information, for most adults. Children, sensory scientists, and artists may dwell on sounds and sights longer than the rest of us. But for the majority of adults, it helps to forget the outer form of the sentence to make room in our limited working memory for the next sentence.

But what does it mean to be "conscious of a meaning"? We certainly seem to be aware of some process of comprehension when we hear a sentence, enough to ask, *"What did you just say?"* if we miss some point. But what is it we are aware of when we are aware of meaning? Can we compare conscious meanings to unconscous knowledge? In reading we commonly experience a "click" of comprehension, maybe a moment when we confirm to ourselves that an abstract sentence makes sense. But what is it we are confirming when something clicks?

This may seem to be an odd question, given that you and I are conscious of the topic of this book, which is abstract indeed. How, you might ask, could abstract concepts *not* be conscious in the minds of people who are talking about them? Physicists are surely conscious of abstractions like "electrons," "atomic orbits," "wave-particle duality," and the like, aren't they? Conventional wisdom seems to say so.

Conscious Access to Meaning

Here is a contrastive experiment that seems to manipulate conscious access to meaning. It indicates that we need working memory in order to stay conscious of the meaning of a sentence.

First, take another look at the paragraph in the preceding section that begins But what does it mean to be "conscious of a meaning"? Reread it in your usual way, with conscious understanding. Now remember these numbers: 11, 47, and 23. Keep them in mind, and read the paragraph again.

For myself, I cannot seem to understand the meaning of the paragraph and keep the three numbers in mind at the same time. To retain the numbers I must rehearse them, and then I can't seem to understand more than a few printed words at a time. It's interesting to go back and forth a few times between normal and "memory-loaded" reading, to explore the difference.

This is a case, of course, of a phenomenal contrast as described in chapter 1. The paragraph you read is the same both times; the action of reading is similar; but some level of interpretation seems consciously inaccessible when you try to hold numbers in immediate memory. What is the difference? It seems to be conscious access to meaning, doesn't it?

Prototypes

What comes to mind when you read these words? Give each one a little time to "sink in."

bird
chair
animal
robber
woman
vegetable

If you are like most people, these names for abstract categories will bring to mind, not an abstract definition, but a specific mental image. As Eleanor Rosch and her coworkers have shown, much of our abstract thinking is encoded in imageable "prototypes." The class of birds is represented not so much by an abstract description of birds, but rather by some *particular* bird we can visualize, like a robin. Similarly, the class of chairs is often mentally represented by the classical kitchen chair, made of wood, with a square back and seat, and with the natural wood grain showing through the finish. This prototype is not the average chair we encounter, nor is it an adequate abstract description of all chairs. Instead, it is something we can conveniently make conscious. Prototypical images serve to index abstract descriptions that cannot be visualized.

What about concepts that are more abstract than birds and chairs? Consider the three words listed below, one by one. What reportable events come to mind when you dwell on each one for about ten seconds?

democracy
popularity
mathematics

Given "democracy," many people educated in the United States report fragmentary associative flashes of American flags, of people standing in line to vote, or pictures of the American Revolution. The exact and complete meaning of "democracy" is of course not captured by such fragmentary images, which may be memories of early schoolbook pictures. The visual fragments do not constitute the whole meaning, just as the prototypical image of a robin is not the same as the complex semantic network needed to understand the concept "bird." Nonetheless, abstract concepts may be easier to manipulate and understand when they have some conscious "handle." The ubiquity of such imageable handles for abstract terms suggests that they are very useful in our mental life.

Thus, one interesting possibility is that many concepts are *accessed* by means of images, or perhaps by conscious words in inner speech.

Even the most abstract concepts may have qualitative mental "access images" of some kind. This hypothesis was popular after 1900 among psychologists who were impressed by the fragmentary and fleeting mental images that often come with abstractions. It has also been advanced by highly creative people like Einstein and Mozart writing about their own mental processes.

Imageable handles for abstractions could explain many things: for example, the extraordinary power of imagery in memory and emotion. Advertising people and political propagandists alike place great faith in the power of emotionally compelling images, and the available research suggests they are right. Try thinking a fearful thought—jumping from a tall building, for example—in words only, and there will be little emotional reaction. But bring up a vivid mental image of jumping, and your heart rate will go up, your sweat glands begin to work, and your body will prepare itself for emergency action. Imagery may also have implications for the power of social stereotypes: prejudice may consist of having standardized, uncomplimentary mental images of a despised group. In the realm of thinking, geometry has had great impact in mathematics, even though we have known since Descartes that all geometrical figures can be expressed algebraically. But geometric graphs can be visualized, while the abstract meaning of algebraic equations cannot. Such qualitative conscious experiences help us to manipulate abstract entities that might otherwise elude our grasp.

Cognitive linguists George Lakoff and Mark Johnson have opened up a great body of evidence indicating that human beings in many cultures use a limited number of metaphors to think about self, other, space and time (1980). They take the view that figures of speech are not just rough approximations to abstract thought, but that they serve as fundamental vehicles for thought. Judging by everyday language we can make a respectable case that much of the time human beings fly on the wings of metaphor—at least until we crash. More accurately perhaps, we use one metaphor as long as it suits us, and hop onto another one when we need to express a different point of view.

One advantage of metaphor is that it connects vague abstractions to a solid perceptual grounding. Here are some examples cited by Lakoff and Johnson. Many cultures use metaphors for love such as *He was burning with love, I am crazy about her, We are one, I was given new strength by her love, The magic is gone, Don't ever let me go, She pursued him relentlessly,* and so on. Some of these figures of speech may bring to mind actual prototypical situations; *He was burning with love* may recall a pubertal occasion when intense love felt uncomfortably "hot" in some close-to-literal sense. But of course we use the figurative expressions far beyond whatever experiences they may resemble.

Many metaphors reflect the same underlying image. For example, cognitive psychologist Raymond Gibbs cites "LOVE AS A NUTRIENT" metaphors: *I was given new strength by her love, I thrive on love, He's sustained by love,* and *I'm starved for your affection.* He writes,

> The LOVE AS A NUTRIENT conceptual metaphor has as its primary function the cognitive role of understanding one concept (love) in terms of another (nutrients). Conceptual metaphors arise when we try to understand difficult, complex, abstract, or less delineated concepts, such as love, in terms of familiar ideas such as nutrients. [Gibbs, 1994, p. 147]

It seems that standard metaphors use images to stand for more abstract realities, as if we take whatever is clearest and most compelling in conscious experience and use it to understand more complicated things. Such perceptual metaphors may be the norm and not the exception in our mental lives.

Most abstract terms evolved from concrete ancestral words fairly recently. In physics, the word "force" did not originate with Newton's insight that F=ma. It began with the notion of military might, the force of armies. By the 20th century and relativity theory, even Newton's abstract concept of force has thinned and vaporized to the vanishing point, so that "force" as an entity ceases to exist. It becomes a mere byproduct of the bending of light by great astronomical masses in space. In the same way, most of us still think of "particles" as tiny objects, when for decades now physicists have found it necessary to postulate "particles" with no mass, no singular location in space, and little or no duration in time. In the quantum ground state there are no "things" at all, simply the probabilistic fluctuation of potentialities. In science, concepts routinely make the journey from perceptual objects to increasingly subtle abstractions, far from the sensory ground of experience.

The journey into abstraction is not limited to formal science. Take such everyday terms as "quality." The philologist Owen Barlow noted that,

> "The word quality is used by most educated people every day of their lives, yet in order that we should have this simple word Plato had to make the tremendous effort of turning a vague feeling into a clear thought. He invented the new word "poiotēs",. . . ."Of-what-kind-ness"

and Cicero translated it by the Latin "qualitas," from "qualis." Language becomes a different thing for us altogether if we can. . . Realize (that) every time the word quality is used. . . That creative effort made by Plato comes into play again."

Of course in English we have lost the sources of latinate terms like quality and quantity, though we have not lost the concrete meanings of "force," "particles," and many other terms based on English originals. Somehow the concrete sensory meaning can live side by side with the abstract one, and the result is not confusion but a fine tool for thinking with clarity.

Such abstractions as time, love, and self are approached with undisguised perceptual metaphors. According to Lakoff and Johnson, time is universally viewed as a journey in which we see someone—ourselves perhaps—walking along a footpath toward the future and away from the past. Love seems to be understood across many cultures in terms of a small number of metaphors, a journey, a partnership, a unification of two selves, a heated experience, a capture, a sustaining source of food. Some of these metaphors may be grounded in everyday sensory experiences.

Scientific ideas that can be expressed in literal formulae still use visual analogues much of the time. Feynman diagrams, invented by the theoretical physicist Richard Feynman to show the differential equations of particle histories in a visual displays with points and arrows, are a good example. Cognitive scientists studying the expertise of physicists and engineers have been surprised to find that the nineteenth-century metaphor of electrical current, like the current of a babbling brook, still dominates much thinking about electricity, even among experts. Physicists may think of atoms in terms of the standard classroom diagram of a visible nucleus surrounded by orbital shells, not in terms of an invisible nucleus, a tiny core of particles surrounded by vast empty space, and far outside, a probability distribution of electron orbits. Years of copying drawings from classroom blackboards and textbooks may give physics students some ready visual images to help concretize equations.

A plausible case can be made for perceptual and imagistic handles on abstract concepts, and in the case of love we may have no better basis than metaphor. Yet abstractions do transcend metaphors in interesting ways—if only because abstract knowledge can freely skip among a variety of different figures of speech. An engineer may "see" the electrical current flowing from one point to another, but as the electrons enter a computer chip, the flow metaphor no longer works; perhaps an image of a circuit diagram takes over at that point. To understand the difference between an electrically conductive metal and a resistive plastic, a mental image of roly-poly atomic nuclei with loosely bound electrons may come to mind for the metal, and tightly bound molecular bonds for the plastic.

That still leaves plenty of possibilities for figurative speech to lead us astray. Metaphors can be very misleading. The history of science is filled with metaphors that explained some observations but then blocked further thought. Psychologists are familiar with the use and abuse of the "steam vessel" metaphor for emotion, which seems to guide many amateur psychotherapists. We know that "blowing off steam" has a ready interpretation when someone expresses suppressed anger with great intensity; it is often followed by a feeling of relief. But Freud's idea that a psychic equivalent to a steam vessel provides all the energy for bodily motion is no longer taken seriously, and there is indeed hard evidence that cultivating the habit of expressing anger does *not* lead to a more peaceful mental life. Just the opposite. The clinical researcher Seymour Feshbach established some years ago that frequent deliberate practice in expressing anger only teaches people to express anger *more often*. In this respect the steam kettle metaphor actually leads to *less* adaptive behavior when it is used for more than obtaining that moment of relief. Metaphors are powerful, but literal knowledge is needed to keep them in touch with reality. A useful caution in this book!

Fragmentary Images

Quickly now, what is going on behind your head? You can't see it, you cannot hear it or feel it, but have you seen a cat quickly whip around to see if it was being stalked by an enemy? Even animals with mainly sensory consciousness must be able to think about events outside the sensory field. A herd of zebras on the Serengeti plains must be able to think somehow about that group of lionesses that faded from sight a minute ago. Where did they go so suddenly? Are they now stalking closer through the tall grass? Zebras must keep track of such invisible things. Do they experience a sudden image of the missing lions? We don't know. But the question is interesting for the avenues of thought it opens up.

Sigmund Freud proposed an explanation for the human tendency of avoiding trains of thought that might lead to intolerable shame or anxiety. He suggested that when we come close to an intolerable thought we might experience "signal anxiety," a fragmentary image of the anxiety-provoking idea, almost as if a mental stop sign was posted at certain choice-points in the stream of thought.

Shakespeare said it better. As King Lear is raging through the stormy night in Act 3, Scene 4, having been shut out by his elder daughters Regan and Goneril, he is urged by the loyal Kent to take shelter in a peasant's hovel. He refuses:

> Thou think'st 'tis much that this contentious storm
> Invades us to the skin: so 'tis to thee;
> But where the greater malady is fix'd,
> The lesser is scarce felt.
>
> . . .
>
> this tempest in my mind
> Doth from my senses take all feeling else,
> Save what beats there—Filial ingratitude!
>
> . . .
>
> In such a night
> To shut me out? Pour on; I will endure.
>
> . . .
>
> Your old kind father, whose frank heart gave all—
> *O, that way madness lies,* let me shun that!
> No more of that.
>
> [italics added]

The psychological question is, *How did Lear know which way madness lies, so as to avoid it?* It is a question that has been raised not just by Shakespeare and Freud, but also in cognitive therapy. Someone suffering from a fear of heights may learn to avoid thinking about tall buildings, for example. But how does a phobic know what thoughts to avoid before they become conscious? The possible use of fragmentary warning images was debated in psychological circles before behaviorism quenched the debate. One common idea was that we might have anticipatory conscious fragments of trains of thought we want to avoid. Thus King Lear could rage against his faithless daughters without fear, but when he allowed himself to contemplate "Your old kind father, whose frank heart gave all—" his emotions threatened to overwhelm him.

Albert Einstein suggested along similar lines that fragmentary visual and muscular images allow the manipulation of more symbols than would be possible in clear consciousness. Those quasi-conscious "handles" may be vague, but in creative thinking they may be more useful than fully conscious terms, which would take up more of our limited capacity (Ghiselin, 1949).

The Advantage of Ideas

Conscious ideas empower us to transcend the sensory moment. They enlarge the fleeting present to minutes, hours, seasons, and lifetimes. Instead of the immediate sensory field, conceptual thoughts gives us access to a vast geographical world that we can know about but cannot experience at any given time. Conscious thinking gives us access to the first moments of the universe, the vastness of evolutionary time, the unknowable tunneling of a probabilistic electron from one energy state to another.

Abstract concepts may be in focal consciousness, but we still typically cannot describe our *experience* of a concept. You can experience a focal conscious image of today's breakfast, or a novel image about a pink elephant, and other perceptual or imaginary events. We can apparently pay focal attention to abstract concepts that are topical. Yet these concepts are "vague" at best. Awareness of beliefs and ideas seems to be a different sort of thing. Such abstract mental events do not have clear perceptual qualities; they have no obvious color, texture, or flavor. If there are fleeting fragments of images associated with them, they are not at all easy to retrieve. Concepts have a mental reality, no question about it. But they may ride on fragments of conscious images, basic brain elements that allow us to use the ancestral sensorimotor system to think.

Some Remarkable Similarities between Sensations and Ideas

One could easily emphasize the great differences between conscious perceptual experiences or images on the one hand and abstract concepts on the other. Abstract ideas like *causality* may be useful fictions; they may be artificial connections between conscious sensory experiences, as skeptical philosophers like David Hume maintained. Concepts may be linguistic creations that allow us to pretend we are dealing with an extended perceptual world, as if there is such a thing as time, cause, or memory. In particle physics, subnuclear particles have now lost all relation to place, time, and mass: is it possible that they were mere perceptual fantasies in the first place?

The only trouble with such a view psychologically is that concepts behave much as percepts do in the theater of mind. They take up limited capacity just like percepts and images; conscious concepts are always internally consistent, like perceptual experiences; and they occur one after the other, serially, just as the other actors speak and move on stage. Consider the evidence.

In the demonstration of the contrastive method earlier in this chapter we asked you to keep in mind three numbers—11, 47, and 23—and notice that as you read a paragraph with loaded working memory that conscious access to its meaning seems to be lost. That is a "limited-capacity" effect—that is, it shows competition between very different conscious contents, numbers and meanings. We can easily show similar spillovers when we load limited capacity with visual images or words. Meaning, words, numbers, and images drive each other out of consciousness when we load our limited capacity. Concepts, which seem to have no perceptual qualities, and auditory words, which do, both have to fit into the bottleneck of limited capacity.

Concepts and percepts both need to be internally consistent. In Chapter 1 we noticed that *Mary had a little lamb* makes for a coherent, understandable conscious flow, while a scrambled sentence such as *had lamb little Mary a* does not. Conscious meanings obey an *internal consistency constraint*. The most obvious example involves ambiguous words: Can you keep more than one meaning of "fix," "bread," or "set" in mind, even for an instant? But there is good evidence that multiple interpretations of ambiguous words exist in the brain, at least unconsciously, for a few hundred milliseconds after input.

Figure 3-4 illustrates the consistency of conscious experience in visual perception. The reversible cube (a) is the famous Necker Cube, which can be experienced in two different ways. With a little practice you can learn to flip it back and forth mentally, almost at will. Part (b) is called the Bookend Illusion, and can be thought of as the smallest reversible part of the Necker Cube. Most people find it easy to see in two different ways. Part (c) is the sinister Devil's Pitchfork, an impossible figure that looks from a distance as if it is coherent—but trace its lines with your eyes, and your visual brain gets into trouble. The Netherlands artist M. C. Escher is famous for his infinite staircases, reversible toads, and impossible buildings, all based on our inability to keep two inconsistent perceptual experiences in mind at the same time. All these examples make the same point: *No matter what we do, the visual system tries to find a single coherent conscious interpretation at any given moment.*

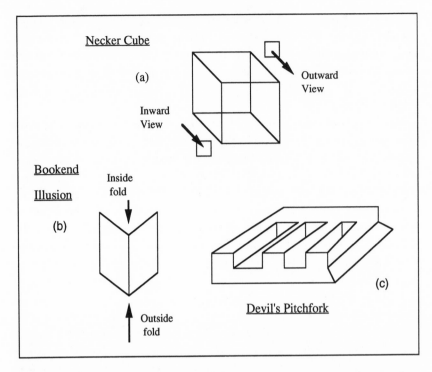

Figure 3-4. *The internal consistency of conscious experience.* At any given moment we are conscious of only one consistent interpretation of conscious events. The Necker Cube and Bookend Illusion can each be experienced in two different ways, but never at the same time. The Devil's Pitchfork is an "impossible figure," which cannot become conscious as a coherent whole, because it contains self-contradictory information. This need for consistency does not seem to apply to unconscious representations, such as the multiple meanings of common words that are known to be activated in reading a sentence like this one. (Baars, 1988)

Fusing Sensory Inputs

Internal consistency is a basic property of conscious experience, but the raw input to the brain may not start off as consistent. Toward the end of the nineteenth century the stereopticon became a popular toy in Victorian parlors. It allowed people to see two photographic slides, one for each eye, taken from slightly different angles. If two photos of a parrot in a cage are taken an inch or so apart, the viewer will get a sensation of depth. Increased separation between the two eyes' views gives an illusion of visual depth that is intensified to surrealistic dimensions, as if seen through a giant's eyes many feet apart from each other. These are all examples of *binocular fusion*, making a coherent conscious experience out of two slightly different inputs.

Under normal conditions two visual streams work together to create a fused visual experience. But binocular fusion breaks down if there are significant differences between the input to the two eyes. As we know, if one image is slightly offset from the other, binocular rivalry results, and to obtain coherence the visual system will suppress one image in favor of another. Using video techniques we can lag one flow of images behind another, and binocular fusion will break down very fast, in a fraction of a second of lag time. In the same way, auditory fusion breaks down if one stream of music, for example, lags the other by more than a tenth of a second. Any significant disparity between the two eyes or ears causes one of the two flows to be suppressed. Conscious perception is always coherent, even if the nervous system needs to cancel some input in favor of another.

It seems that inputs to the two eyes either compete or cooperate, and the same is true of the two ears, or even two parts of the skin. Two decades ago Georg Békésy, a Nobelist in sensory physiology at Harvard University, found that when symmetrical points on the two knees are rhythmically vibrated at the same time, we experience a common vibrating source somewhere in the middle! But fusion breaks down when we speak into a device that imposes a short time lag before we can hear our own voice; such delayed auditory feedback makes speaking essentially impossible. We need vocal feedback to control normal speech, just as we need to feel solid ground when we step out on an icy day. But feedback delayed is worse than no feedback at all. Under ordinary circumstances in walking, the flow of visual perspectives, the feeling of our feet, and the sounds of our footsteps work together to create a single conscious reality.

In general, it seems to be impossible for human beings to hold two different interpretations of the same thing in consciousness at the same time. In many cases we can prove that two representations exist fleetingly in the brain, but only one can be conscious at a time.

Different ideas as well as percepts seem to come one after the other; if that were not so, you might be able to absorb this book in a few large mental bites. That is only possible if you are so thoroughly familiar with the ideas in this book that you could handle them automatically. But as long as input contains large amounts of unpredictable information, the human head is held to serial consciousness.

In sum, it seems that ideas and sensations share many basic features: They occur one after the other (serially); they are unified, or rather, internally consistent; when they are not consistent with each other, they will compete against each other for access to consciousness; both may trigger voluntary actions; and so on. In other words, ideas and sensations seem like two different experiences that make use of the same mental faculty of consciousness.

Many Conscious Events Seem To Have Simultaneous Sensory and Abstract Character

One of the wonderful characteristics of language is that we seem to be aware of both sound and meaning, pretty much at the same time. It is easy to show this with Lewis Carroll's "Jabberwocky," in which we see letters, words, morphemes, and syntax all operating without meaning.

> 'Twas brillig, and the slithy toves
> did gyre and gimble in the wabe;
> all mimsy were the borogoves
> and the mome raths outgrabe.

It would seem that we can have at least two levels of experience, though we cannot rule out the possibility that consciousness may be rapidly switching back and forth between the two.

Such a multileveled experience would appear to contradict the claim made above that sensations and ideas tend to compete against each other. I do not know of formal research to resolve this point. It may be that we can handle two levels, perception and meaning, if they are consistent with each other, just as we can handle two streams of visual or auditory information when they are mutually consistent.

The multilayered nature of experience is not limited to language. Human interactions seem to have a beginning, a middle, and an end, but much of that may be in the mind of the beholder. When little Susie and Mary are fighting, Susie will tell the story starting from Mary stealing her bicycle, while Mary will begin the narrative at a different point, when Susie first called her a bad name. In court testimony, eyewitnesses predictably tell quite different stories about the same human interactions.

The boundaries of sensory experience may also be imposed. Here is a trite but effective demonstration of an unchanging sensory event with a change in word form. Where are the word boundaries in this example?

AYESKREEMYOUSKREEMWEALLSKREEMF'RAYESKREEM

Notice that it begins and ends in ayeskreem, sliced up at different points. The first is aye/skreem, and the second, ayes/kreem. There are no physical word boundaries, of course, just as in normal speech we do not insert little pauses between spoken words. But we humans still *experience* such nonexistent boundaries in the flow of speech. The experience of nonexistent *units* seems to add an abstract layer to conscious experience, separate from the simple sensory event. It is a kind of overlay that we impose upon the words we hear and the events we see.

Even when we are conscious of a coffee cup we may actually be experiencing not one but several layers of visual representation, super-imposed on each other. A useful analogy is a set of transparent over-lays of a geological map, one showing the altitude of hills and valleys, another vegetation, and a third streams and lakes, all in contrasting colors. When the transparent overlays are superimposed on each other, you can see them all together. In looking at the cup of coffee you can then focus at will on the hue of tiny parts of the cup, on textures, out-lines, shapes, shadows and reflections, even on a single point of light captured by a surface irregularity of the glazing. And yet, you also see the cup as an object, and a useful one at that. Each of these features is processed by a different part of the visual brain, yet all can be simulta-neously appreciated when we look at the cup; all layers seem to be reflected in consciousness at the same time.

Artists often feel hemmed in by the layers of conventional interpre-tation that we impose on visual experiences, and they have found sim-ple ways to break up conventionalized experience, to "make it strange." Look at a familiar face upside down, and it will lose much of its famil-iarity. You can see it in a mirror, sideways, or against an unfamiliar background. Or we can try the opposite, and gaze at an object until all that sense of its being known seems to fade. We can zoom in on details to break up its wholeness, or blow it up to some impossible size. The question is, or course, how does the brain create a single conscious experience from many layers of input?

Separating an Object from Its Meaning

Much of our understanding of the brain began with the careful study of impairments due to stroke or injury by pioneering neurologists. But in the last ten or twenty years our ability to analyze very subtle losses has grown remarkably. Patients have been found who lack just one level of visual analysis, such as face recognition, or even visual facial knowl-edge of only a single person. Some stroke victims lack only one aspect of language, such as the ability to understand animate nouns or syntactic function words like "and," "or," and "by." These cases provide a primary source of evidence that the brain is a collection of highly specialized unconscious experts, autonomous audience members in the theater of consciousness.

Visual agnosia is another significant disorder, in which conscious object perception is intact, but the *meaning* of the object is lost. Patients can tell the color, shape, and pattern of the coffee cup, but not what it is for.

Here is a demonstration of a remarkable phenomenon—a safe and reversible analogue of agnosia.

Semantic Satiation

1. Simply repeat a single word to yourself over and over again for half a minute. Repeat the word "satiation," for example. . . .

What did you experience?

2. Most people report a distinct loss of meaning after only a small number of repetitions. "Semantic satiation" is a metaphor of sorts, of course, as if neurons are little creatures to be filled up with the word until their little bellies are full, they are sated and want no more. Even single neurons habituate; that is, they stop firing to a repetitive pattern of stimulation. But semantic satiation affects our conscious experience, not just individual neurons.

Is the word "satiation" more meaningful again? The image of neurons filling their little bellies until they are full was intended to create a visual context for the word, to make it meaningful again. How does it seem at this moment? More meaningful?

3. Now try repeating "satiation" until it satiates again. . . .

Has it lost meaning again.

4. Semantic satiation has held great fascination for psychologists since Gestalt psychology of the 1920s, but it has not led to much research. It is just one of those intriguing things that we know about, full of interesting resonances, but resistant to experimental analysis. One question you are testing right now is whether the word "satiation" recovers its meaning when we put it back into some meaningful context. For example, we can tell you that semantic satiation is a *redundancy effect*—one of many cases where a repeated experience can cause a loss of conscious access and organization. Redundancy effects exist in every sense modality and at every level of complexity. The eye normally protects itself against redundancy with a constant tremor, but if we construct a special apparatus to project a single stable image on the

retina for more than a few seconds, awareness of the image simply disappears. Redundant information fades from consciousness. It is one more contrast between matched conscious and unconscious representations.

Now, has the paragraph above reinstated the meaning of "satiation" to some extent? If this demonstration worked for you, you should experience both *meaning lost* and *meaning regained*. Sheer repetition (Steps 1. and 3.) should make the meaning fade, but adding new meaningful connections (Steps 2. and 4.) should make it come alive again. What was your experience? Repeating a word and reinstating its meaning both involve phenomenological contrasts, of course. They provide yet another empirical boundary for understanding conscious experience.

In Sum

Sensory consciousness seems to be special. It gives us our most vivid moment-to-moment experiences. Mental images seem to be "faint copies" of sensory events, generated from within the brain itself. As far as the brain is concerned, sensations and images belong together. Abstract ideas, on the other hand, allow us to transcend the limitations of the perceptual world in time and space, to enter the many realms of abstraction. Concepts do not have the same compelling sense of conscious reality as percepts do because they have no qualia—no reds and greens, no stubble and wetness, no smell. The parts of the human cortex that support abstract thinking seem relatively recent on an evolutionary scale, and may ride on the older functioning of sensory cortex. Having said all that, we cannot forget that in language, in interpreting other people, in music and art, we often combine the sensory and the abstract into a single, seamless flow of experience.

Further Reading

Semir Zeki's *A Vision of the Brain* (1993) is a very up-to-date book on the visual brain from a leading researcher. Perceptual psychologist Irving Rock's book *Perception* (1984) is an excellent introduction, and Richard Gregory's classic *Eye and Brain* (1966) is still essential reading. A good account of psycholinguistics can be found in Steven Pinker's *Language Instinct: How the Mind Creates Language* (1994). Arthur Reber's *Implicit Learning* (1993) will likely become a classic description of the kind of learning that is involved in acquiring language, in which the regularities that are learned apparently never become conscious. An overview of the role of metaphor in thinking is provided by George Lakoff's (1987) *Women, Fire, and Other Dangerous Things: What Categories Reveal About the Mind.*

four

THE SPOTLIGHT:
ATTENTION, ABSORPTION, AND
THE CONSTRUCTION OF REALITY

Everyone knows what attention is. It is the taking possession by
the mind, in clear and vivid form, of one out of what seem several
simultaneously possible objects or trains of thought. Focalization,
concentration of consciousness are its essence.

WILLIAM JAMES, THE PRINCIPLES OF PSYCHOLOGY (1890)

William James believed that attention is a selective capacity
that results in conscious experience, much as the movements of a spotlight result in light falling on a particular
actor. Thus attention is a selective act that results in a conscious event.
The distinction between selective attention and the resulting conscious
experience helps clarify many puzzling questions. Attentional selection
is guided by many conscious and unconscious factors.

Given our inclination to pay attention only to selected parts of the
world, how is it that we stay in touch with reality? The conscious flow
is *constructed so as to make sense of almost any consistent input,* as we
can see in dreams and brain damage. Dreams appear in response to
random stimulation from the brain stem, which the cortex interprets
with remarkably creative, fluid, and vivid imagery, *ad hoc* stories that
flow free of any sensory constraint; and brain damage often shows people struggling to create coherence in a broken world, patching over the
missing pieces with remarkable facility. In reading a novel or watching a

play, we often enter absorbed states of mind in which we seem to accept whole fictional worlds without difficulty.

But contrary to some popular views, consciousness does not allow an easy escape from reality. Even when we are absorbed in one flow of experiences the brain remains exquisitely sensitive to biologically and personally significant events going on outside of consciousness. Whenever a significant event is detected, a great tidal wave of neural activity sweeps through the entire brain. Thus, significant anomalies often break through to consciousness even if we try to avoid them, and once conscious, anomalous events trigger numerous problem-solving mechanisms. There is an unforgiving reality out there that the brain has evolved to deal with, and consciousness seems to be our primary means for adapting to it.

Cognitive scientists tend to study reasoning. We have learned a great deal from studies of people performing mental calculations, playing chess and solving puzzles, but most of the time we humans do not engage in logical or even structured thinking. We can do it, but it is something of a feat. Social and clinical psychologists are much closer to common sense in that regard: Their evidence shows that we humans devote most of our conscious stream to fantasies, dreams, disconnected thoughts, and debatable beliefs. The stream of consciousness, as William James wrote famously, seems a messy, arbitrary sort of thing, full of stops and starts, hopping and skipping from one half-articulated thought to another. For most of human history that has been the norm. Structured reasoning is a recent cultural product.

People are wonderfully sensitive to accurate reasoning and reality when they are provided with rapid and accurate consequences. We do not walk into tables and walls; and we are remarkably successful hunters, weavers, gatherers, cooks, spinners, farmers, and engineers. Over time, we have acquired truthful beliefs even about invisible things like atoms and black holes. But wherever we cannot obtain clear reality feedback we seem to spin beliefs that are contradictory, idiosyncratic, and fantastical. Any situation that does not provide rapid and accurate reality monitoring is an invitation to fantasy.

Consider how many sources of information in everyday life are plainly unreliable. We are pretty sure about our immediate sensory surroundings most of the time, and in the modern world we have good information about the world beyond our senses. But we cannot read minds, though we depend from infancy on the goodwill of others whose minds we would like to know. We do not know the future, though we are always betting on future outcomes. We do not even know our own past, because human memory is notoriously full of shadowy uncertainties. In the face of even moderate complexity we run into trouble, from finding the right soap in a crowded supermarket aisle to understanding societal change. And when it comes to values—what choices are right and wrong—to guide our actions, there is no objective standard at all; the "shoulds" of life are social constructions. That is tolerable in a traditional society with social constructions that are shared and stable, but in the modern world the absence of agreed-upon values in life creates deep and lasting uncertainties. In sum, uncertainty prevails in our efforts to know the past, the future, other people, ourselves, and anything complex and value-laden. And there is a kind of Law of Expectation, phrased in many different ways by different observers, which states that *whenever we lack certainty about the world, our conscious experience is heavily determined by unsupported expectations*. Reality becomes a Rorschach blot.

Things may be different for hunter-gatherers in the Great African Rift Valley, living close to the level of survival for each day's hunt. Farmers in hardscrabble country, where every moment is driven by the demands of reality, do not seem unduly bothered by existential crises. But in the modern world, where most of us are far removed from the unforgiving demands of a harsh reality, humans seem to be driven at least as much by fantasy as reality. Hours of our lives are spent in wishful or fearful fantasies; like humans everywhere, we enter into a fantastical dream world each night for two hours; and our stream of consciousness appears to be notoriously arbitrary.

These are probably adaptive features of our minds, but it is not at all clear what the evolutionary payoff of a rich fantasy life might be. Do we sustain long-term goals by fantasies of golden rewards? Are we sexier because we have sexual fantasies? And is storytelling a sort of social glue that keeps the human clan together? We just do not know.

The truth seems to be that we are a gullible species whenever we cannot get rapid reality feedback. Most of us fall victim on a regular basis to false beliefs, or worse, to self-serving beliefs peddled by advertisers, politicians, and utopian dreamers. All cultures postulate self-flattering fantasies to try to make more bearable the ineluctable mysteries of death, transitoriness, and suffering. Our self-proclaimed title of *Homo sapiens,* the wise or discerning human, is surely a hope rather than reality. Most of the time we are only *Homo credens,* the species that needs to believe as much as it needs to breathe.

What does all this have to do with consciousness? First, if the Law of Expectation is true, many of our conscious beliefs that seem real may in fact be crucially shaped by our own thoughts. Then, there is evidence that our ability to engage in fantasy depends upon *absorption*, the degree to which we can exclude alternative conscious contents. And finally, the whole business of directing and selecting the stream of consciousness depends upon *attention*.

The Difference between Attention and Consciousness

For forty years scientists have used William James's definition of attention, quoted at the beginning of this chapter. It is routinely cited in scientific writings on attention, and yet, we have not read James's definition as carefully as we should have. James makes a very clear, commonsense distinction between attention and consciousness, but under the influence of behaviorism, researchers over the last four decades have studied attention without dealing clearly with consciousness. As a result, the scientific literature tends to use the words "attention" and "consciousness" interchangeably, as if they mean the same thing. But James clearly believed that attention and consciousness are different, in important ways. Let's look at the famous passage again. The words that are often overlooked are in italics.

> *My experience is those things I agree to attend to,* those items I notice shape my mind—without selective interest, experience is an utter chaos.
>
> Everyone knows what attention is. *It is the taking possession by the mind,* in clear and vivid form, of one out of what seem several simultaneously possible objects or trains of thought. *Focalization, concentration of consciousness* are its essence. [italics added] [1890, p. 380]

For William James, attention is not the same as consciousness; rather, attention involves *selecting* one conscious experience rather than another. We turn the dial to a football game on television *in order to experience it consciously.* Tuning in the game is a selective act: watching it is the resulting conscious experience.

English makes a clear distinction between "looking" versus "seeing," "listening" versus "hearing," "touching" versus "feeling," and maybe even "sniffing" versus "smelling." The first word of each pair imparts a sense of selection, while the second describes the resulting conscious experience. We look in order to see, listen in order to hear, and touch in order to feel.

The spotlight metaphor comes in handy here. In the dark theater we cannot see who controls the spotlight or what decisions guide its movements. All that is hidden in darkness. We only experience the *results* of those decisions. From that point of view attention is not something we normally experience. It is a vast and subtle network of centers located throughout the brain that serve to select and direct information toward consciousness.

Eye movements are guided by part of the extensive attentional network of the brain. At this moment your eyes are moving with exquisite accuracy to those points on the printed line that carry the greatest amount of information. Like other elements of selective attention, the eyes are guided there in order *to select* and *focus* on certain conscious contents. Thus we move our eyes *in order to* make certain things conscious. But it makes no sense to confuse selective eye movements with the resulting consciousness of *this printed phrase.* In exactly the same way it makes no sense to confuse selective attention with the conscious experiences that result from it.

There is an apparent exception to this separation between attention and consciousness. That is the case of conscious attentional decisions, where we experience a moment of choice between reading a book and watching television, for example. Here conscious considerations can obviously influence our decision of what to become conscious of next. The sequence is

1. a conscious decision to pay attention to something, followed by
2. unconscious attentional activity, followed by
3. the targeted conscious contents.

Thus we think about what to watch on television, turn the dial automatically once the decision is made, and then become conscious of the result. Traditionally this has been called voluntary attention, and we will explore it below.

The distinction between attention and consciousness leads to an interesting interpretation of new discoveries by Michael Posner, S.E. Petersen and colleagues. The Posner group localized attentional structures by giving subjects very simple, carefully designed tasks to do, and obtaining PET scans to show high regions of brain activity during specific task components. When subjects were asked to pay attention to some particular aspect of a visual event, several regions in frontal cortex lit up, especially on the inside surface of the hemispheres, just in front

A Unified Image

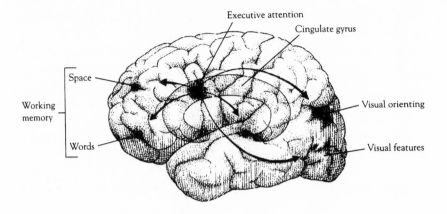

Figure 4-1. *A brain demonstration of the difference between attention and visual consciousness.* In landmark work using cognitive and brain imaging techniques, Michael Posner and his coworkers recently discovered a network of brain centers involved in visual executive attention: Our ability to select different visual targets at will. The attentional network selects what becomes conscious, but it is mostly unconscious itself. Only the "visual features" area at the rear tip of the brain is believed to be conscious. Thus, visual attention *controls access* to visual consciousness, but it is not the same as consciousness.

of the great bridge of fibers that connects the left and right cortexes, the corpus callosum.

Take a close look at Figure 4-1, which represents the results of many hundreds of PET scans. Notice the brain regions involved in the attentional network discovered by Posner and Peterson. If we look from left to right, we see elements of working memory—as when we tell ourselves verbally to pay attention to our left little toes, for example, or simply remember that a ball has just rolled behind a couch. There is an executive attention center in the cingulate gyrus, just above the inside loop connecting the two hemispheres, corresponding to what we will call voluntary attention (discussed in the next section); a visual orienting region in the rear of the brain, involved in shifting attention to and from some particular target; and finally the very rear tip of the brain, labeled "visual features." Remarkably, *only the last region, which includes the early visual projection areas to cortex, is known to directly involve conscious visual experience.*

How do we know that only the visual projection area involves visual consciousness? Chapter 3 cited four sources of evidence. First, when area V1 is lost, people report a loss of visual conscious experience, though they can still "guess" at the objects their eyes are looking at. Second, when the early visual areas are stimulated by a gentle current, people report conscious visual flashes (phosphemes). Third, when people are conscious of a visual object, we can see the early visual areas "light up" in PET scans, indicating a distinct increase in neural activity. Fourth, recording of single cells in visual cortex indicates that there is a difference between the conscious and unconscious flow of stimulation, using competing streams of visual flow to the two eyes. Together these four sources of evidence provide strong support for the hypothesis that the early visual projection areas are critical for visual consciousness. None of these facts apply to the other attentional areas.

We could not make sense of these findings without making a clear distinction between attention and consciousness. It is a distinction that fits common sense—being embedded in the vocabulary of everyday language—as well as a large body of scientific findings. And we now know it also fits recent findings based on real-time imaging of the living brain.

Thinking about Thinking: Voluntary Attention Requires Metacognition

Most shifts of attention are not under moment-to-moment voluntary control. But to decide whether to pay attention to one thing rather than another, we need some knowledge about the things that could potentially become conscious. Every child knows of the heroic struggle between wanting to play outside with your friends and plodding through your homework. It is a hard struggle, and it could not exist without the ability to consciously imagine the alternatives. Voluntary attention seems to involve that ability.

To select one or the other conscious event we need to think about our own mental processes, a feat called *metacognition*. Metacognition is an area of research in its own right; it is of great importance in school performance, eyewitness identification in the courts, and training people to cope with brain damage. Students tend to underestimate the amount of conscious study needed to really understand some material, and sometimes they spend too much time studying unimportant things. These are both problems in metacognition, and there is evidence that learning to make better metacognitive judgments improves school performance.

What does it mean to be conscious of the ability to make a choice? Obviously it is not the same as consciousness of some singular sensory event, because the choices we can imagine making are potential, they are abstract (Chapter 3). In reality, we may never finish our homework, or worse, we may never have a chance to go outside to play; they are only thoughts.

A great deal is known about decision processes, but there has been little research into the conscious experience of the moment of making a choice. It may be difficult to obtain reliable reports of whatever experience there may be of the moment of a decision, and yet, most of us would confidently say that we do make many conscious choices. Since the nineteenth century we have known that choice reaction time—the time it takes to choose between event A or B—takes several times as long as simple reaction time, the time to respond to A all by itself. The more choices we have, the longer it takes to respond. But that bare fact only suggests what we already know: that making choices involves the conscious limited-capacity system. When the appearance of A or B is completely predictable, responses can be handled automatically and unconsciously. If mental options were represented purely unconsciously—in the audience of the theater—there would be no competition between different processes. The increased time needed to make choices seems to reflect the great bottleneck of the mind, the limited-capacity system that is so closely tied to conscious experience.

Metacognition and Overload

If a commercial on television proclaims that "Brand A soap is better than Brand B" we need to do a little more thinking to entertain the possibility that the statement may not be true. A thought like "That idea is false" is inherently metacognitive. It refers to another thought.

Now here is a tricky point. Conscious metacognition loads the limited capacity system just like any conscious task does, as we can easily show by asking people to make some metacognitive decision—how long do you want to watch this television show? for example—while keeping six arbitrary numbers in working memory. Obviously we will see interference between the two tasks, which is just what we mean when we say that conscious metacognition "loads limited capacity."

What if we need to do some metacognitive task when our working memory is already completely loaded? Tasks that require more capacity than is available simply fall off the apple cart. In an overload situation, metacognition will be impaired or impossible, and all the activities that require metacognition—self-monitoring, skepticism, deciding what to pay attention to next—may be lost.

This is not an unusual occurrence. In fact, it is exactly what seems to be happening in an everyday state of mind called *absorption*—with profound and unexpected consequences.

Absorption and Suspension of Disbelief

Several times a day all of us enter mental states that are uninterrupted for minutes or hours: we may become enthralled by a book or creative project, or just engage in a psychologically demanding task, like writing or shadowing speech. In absorbed states, people

1. resist interruption;
2. tend to lose track of time;
3. have decreased self-awareness;
4. tend to suspend disbelief; and
5. become passive about what to pay attention to.

Absorption has all the earmarks of low metacognition, probably because metacognitive thinking is simply pushed out of immediate memory by the absorbing flow of events.

Fiction, we are told by literary scholars, operates by means of a "willing suspension of disbelief." We live for a while in the world evoked by an author or playwright. How do we come to do such a sophisticated thing without knowing which mental switch to throw in order to suspend disbelief or how to scramble back to adult realism when we need to? If disbelief is a conscious disputing of some previous conscious contents—telling ourselves, *No, that can't be true*—it is easy to see how absorption might lead us to suspend skeptical questioning. We need only suppose that disbelief takes up limited capacity. If other conscious contents have higher priority than disbelief, it must logically fall by the wayside. By soaking up the entire limited capacity of consciousness and working memory, *absorption may make it momentarily impossible to disbelieve*. It allows us for a while to live in wishful fantasy.

It is interesting in this connection that there is a significant correlation between the traits of absorption and suggestibility. And "suggestibility," in turn, is a better word for that great mystery, the puzzle of hypnosis.

Suggestion:
The Power of Unopposed, Conscious Ideas

Hypnosis, we are told by researchers who have investigated the topic for decades, does not exist. There are many indications of this. One is the arbitrariness of the induction rituals that lead to "hypnosis": none of the commonly used hypnotic rituals are necessary. Susceptible people will meet all the criteria for "hypnosis" even without the ritual of fixating on a pendulum, rolling the eyes up into their orbits, or raising one's arm; indeed, for the most susceptible fifth of the population, these rituals do not improve performance at all. For the highly suggestible among us, anything that is believed to create "hypnosis" will do so. Hearing a randomly chosen word in a conversation will work quite well. Further, suggestibility takes place without trance; there is no known physiological state that accompanies high suggestibility; and no authoritative hypnotist is needed.

Suggestible states are very commonplace. Medical students who study frightening diseases for the first time routinely develop vivid delusions of having the "disease of the week"—whatever they are currently studying. This temporary kind of hypochondria is so common that it has acquired a name, "medical student syndrome." In drug studies we always need to compare the active treatment being tested to a placebo group, a comparison group that is given fake treatment, like a sugar pill. Placebo comparisons are mandatory because the effects of suggestion are so pervasive and powerful in medical research. For instance, it seems to be generally true that medications in capsules are more effective than the identical substance in tablet form; the painkilling effects of morphine are more than half due to suggestion. Hundreds of other common experiences are deeply influenced by suggestion. In injuries, the intensity of conscious pain and suffering is very susceptible to suggestion.

If hypnosis does not exist as a distinct entity, what is it that happens to people in that unnamed situation? Many researchers prefer just to be descriptive and call it *high suggestibility* without implying anything odd or mysterious. Suggestibility may just be an aspect of ordinary "absorbed" consciousness.

How could this be? William James, who knew about this pattern of the evidence about "hypnosis" even in 1890, gave a delightfully simple answer. Guiding our actions, he thought, were conscious goals and ideas. As soon as we become fully absorbed in a mental image of eating that delicious peanut butter and jelly sandwich, we will simply get up, walk to the kitchen, and do it. Only when we have competing thoughts do we inhibit such goal images. James's *ideomotor theory* of voluntary control simply states that consciousness is impulsive; barring contrary thoughts or intentions, conscious goal images and ideas tend to be believed and executed (see Chapter 6).

In modern terms, conscious goals and ideas tend to be carried out "by default." If that is true, suggestion is *merely the ordinary functioning of consciousness without the added mental operation of self-doubt*. The reason why in "hypnosis" we can extend an arm rigidly with unsuspected strength is that we do not entertain doubts about our ability to do it. Presumably in absorbed states there is simply no room for self-doubt, or for any other metacognitive, self-conscious thoughts.

Fortunately, there is a very nice fit between the ideomotor theory and the theater metaphor (see Chapter 6). Messages proclaimed from the stage are able to reach any specialized system in the brain, including those that control action. In absorbed states there are no competing actors and there is nothing to keep the conscious thought from being carried out.

Consciousness and the Construction of Reality

Science fiction writers tell us that in the coming age of virtual reality computers, many of us will have trouble telling the difference between *real* reality and the virtual kind. I've occasionally played with the thought that "reality" might be that part of our experience that people can agree on from many perspectives, to which we can see no alternative, and which does *not* live up to our idealized expectations. No matter what I try mentally, certain stubborn tables and chairs still go on being themselves. So does the flow of traffic on the highway and the price of apples. As for the astonishing perversity of human beings— going their own way in spite of the best efforts of parents, teachers, newspapers, religious tracts, and governments to persuade them to do otherwise . . . But you get the idea. Reality is a humbling sort of thing.

Try as we might, most human beings cannot live full time in a world of fantasy. Virtual reality computers are but the latest invention in the quest for real-seeming fantasies. Many others have been tried before, only to yield ultimately to the real thing. Hallucinogenic drugs, waking fantasies, rituals and myths, dreams, *folies à deux* and *folies à tous*, urban myths and group paranoias, television serials, rumors and fables, spellbinding demagogy and hypnosis, we still come back to everyday existence when we need to earn a living, go to the grocery store, or walk without bumping into things. But there are states in which our capacity for spinning deceptive copies of reality shines through, and they do tell us something about consciousness.

Constructed Realities in Dreams

Antti Revonsuo, a Finnish cognitive scientist, and V. S. Ramachandran, neurologist and experimental psychologist at the University of California in San Diego have independently suggested that dreams may be considered to be *virtual* realities, vivid simulations of the real thing. It is a provocative idea, and it is certainly true that in the absence of sensory input the brain tends to construct vivid experiences that do not match that stubborn down-to-earth reality in the world. It is a bit like the parable of the Chinese sage who dreamt he was a butterfly, and on waking could not tell if he was a sage dreaming of being a butterfly or a butterfly dreaming he was a sage. It is a charming idea, but not one with much survival value. If the sage were spotted by a hungry sparrow, he would have to resolve his identity crisis very quickly.

Even in the waking brain creative construction of reality does occur. Every waking moment we construct a smooth visual reality out of dozens of narrow jumpy snapshots collected over many separate eye fixations. It is instructive to watch someone else's eyes while reading; the eyes are easily seen to jump from fixation to fixation. As it turns out, we are nearly blind during the jumps, as our eyes are moving from point to point. Only the fixations are conscious of a visual object, and of course the amount of visual information we can take in during any given fixation is limited by the size of the fovea. Thus your experience right now of smoothly reading a stable printed page emerges from a great deal of brainwork; it is not there in the raw input. But our normal construction of waking consciousness gives us a very good approximation of the real world, much better than the undigested input provides.

Ordinarily, we can verify visual experiences by touching the world around us, or by tasting, smelling, and listening to it. The senses provide convergent information, helping to strengthen our confidence in the reliability of our experiences. In walking we sprout predictions every single moment about the surfaces we step on. We test our world by manipulating it, and fortunately most of the time our hands and eyes and all the other sensorimotor organs tend to converge on a single stable story. Finally we use other people to test our version of reality, to tell us when we are wrong or too much swayed by personal idiosyncrasies. Waking consciousness does a good job of tracking perceptual reality. It may not work well with untestable beliefs and feelings (see Chapter 3).

Rude Interruptions

Let us suppose that you are utterly absorbed in this book, and therefore not inclined to be interrupted. Now someone calls your name. From studies of two-channel listening, we know that your own name will simply interrupt the flow of absorbed experience. Indeed, any stimulus with personal or biological value will tend to do so: fire alarms, shooting pains, the delicious odor of cooking food, hunger pangs, emotionally charged thoughts of internal origin. Absorption does not protect us from high-priority signals, even those that begin unconsciously.

When something surprising or significant occurs, an orienting response is evoked—a great wave of neural activity, affecting every part of the nervous system. Three hundred milliseconds after a surprising stimulus, a positive tidal wave goes through the EEG. We stop, look and listen, explore whatever surprised us if we can, study it, try to cope with it, run from it if necessary, and in general try to solve whatever problem is being posed by it. The cognitive psychologist Endel Tulving suggests that large parts of the brain, such as the hippocampus, have a primary function of *mismatch-detection:* spotting events that violate our expectations, and triggering attentional mechanisms to direct the surprising events to consciousness.

Consciousness does not allow an easy escape from reality. Even when we are absorbed in one flow of experiences, the brain remains exquisitely sensitive to biologically and personally significant events going on outside of consciousness. There is an unforgiving reality out there that the brain has evolved to deal with, and consciousness seems to be our primary means for adapting to it.

Perchance to Dream

Yet each night, for two hours at least, dreams create a believable version of reality. Freud thought that dreams were created by the need to protect sleep against unacceptable impulses from the unconscious—that "cauldron of seething excitations"—where wishful thoughts and aggressive fantasies lived in riotous splendor. Conflictful thoughts and feelings certainly show up in dreams, but there is no evidence that they *cause* dreams. Based on careful comparisons between species, Jonathan Winson of Rockefeller University has proposed that dreaming goes back at least to early land-dwelling mammals.

The most widely accepted view today is that dreams are triggered by *unpatterned* neural activity arising from deep in the brain stem and flowing up to cortex, which tries desperately to make sense of the meaningless stimulation. Neuroscientist J. Allan Hobson of Harvard Medical School is its main proponent, and it fits a substantial amount of evidence. But Hobson's activation theory does not tell us how dream *contents* arise. Dream experiences are based, we can assume, on whatever imaginative interpretation the cortex is currently prepared to make of its random input. But that means we are back where we started: If cortex is the creator of dreams, and if it shapes them in accord with its dominant expectations, then dreams are a sort of Rorschach inkblot with extraordinary fluid imaginative power, a mental movie with few reality constraints and a plot spun with ad hoc inventiveness. It is the ultimate example of the mind wildly at play with itself.

Hallucinogenic drugs like LSD have a chemical resemblance to serotonin, the neural messenger that mediates dreaming. It is now believed that these drugs mimic serotonin and that LSD experiences are actually fantastical dreams that occur during waking consciousness.

The Conscious Dream

Judging by the overall electrical activity of the brain, dreams are a kind of conscious state, as indeed we can remember afterwards. The EEG in dreaming looks almost exactly like waking consciousness. Its voltage is lower, but the electrical waves are low, fast, and irregular just as they are in normal wakefulness. In contrast, deeply unconscious states like deep sleep and coma are marked by high, slow, and regular waves.

What does this electrical pattern mean? There are several scientific models, but the simplest idea is that the fast, noisy-looking activity of wakefulness all over the brain may show the activity of many independent neurons, much like a loud cocktail party with hundreds of people talking at the same time. If everyone at the party were to start singing the same slow song, over and over again, the loudness graph would appear loud, slow, and regular, just like the EEG of deep sleep and coma. Singing in unison involves much less information than the hubbub of thousands of independent conversations. The anarchic appearance of waking consciousness may show us the neural marketplace of activity, chaotic on the surface but efficient and productive as a whole.

Do dreams involve virtual realities? Most of the time dream content seems real enough. People rarely doubt their own dream narratives, at least not until it breaks down, as bizarre discontinuities appear in the story line. Like most conscious contents, dreams are always *referred outward* to some conceivable world. Dreams appear to be constructed realities in that sense: they have some momentary meaning, plot, characters, action, motivation, and interaction between self and other.

Lucid Dreaming:
Conscious Metacognition during Dreams

Given all the evidence that we are quite conscious during dream states, it is perhaps not surprising that we can also learn to be *self*-conscious. "Lucid dreaming" is one of the most interesting discoveries of the last ten years. It is the ability to think about, signal, and deliberately try to transform a dream *during the dream*. Lucid dreaming is marked by awareness that one is dreaming, and just as you might expect, it involves a skeptical stance toward the reality of the dream. The lucid dream begins with the realization that *this is only a dream*. It is not real. Skepticism is of course an achievement of metacognition.

Stephen LaBerge and William Dement of Stanford University were the first modern workers to explore the possibility of lucid dreaming. In dreams the thick sheath of outer muscles that move our bodies is effectively paralyzed, except for the muscles needed for breathing, eye movements, and a few other things. Visual input is blocked. But the dream state is marked by regular episodes of large, fairly rapid eye movements, about one per second, in sustained bursts. LaBerge and Dement wondered whether dreamers might be able to signal when they hear a tone by moving their eyes back and forth (see Figure 4-2). It turns out that they can; they can also voluntarily suspend breathing and even move a finger in response to a tone. The most important point is not the eye movements themselves, of course, but the fact that *they can be used to communicate a message about the dreamer's experience.* Eye movements can serve as voluntary signals about a conscious event.

What makes ordinary dream reports hard to trust is the long interval between the dream and the dream report. We dream about two hours each night, but remember only a few fragments in the morning. Why some dreams are remembered the next morning is a mystery, and we do not know whether dreams are transformed in the very act of remembering them. It seems likely. Dream reports cannot be accepted on sight; they must be treated with caution.

Lucid dreams help solve this problem because they allow for immediate signals from people in the midst of a dream. The discovery that lucid dreams can be verified was a major step forward. As we see so often, once methodological problems are solved, a world of interesting possibilities opens up.

But the main lesson for us here is the role of metacognition and skepticism, which appears to be necessary if we are not to be drawn

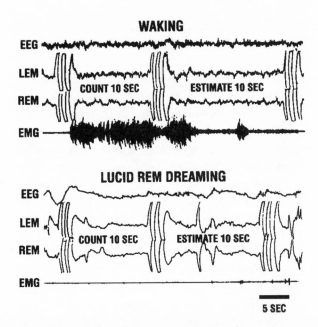

Figure 4-2. *Communicating in the midst of a dream.* Among the most remarkable discoveries of the last decade is *lucid dreaming*, the ability to be aware of one's own dreams. The upper traces show a waking subject silently counting to ten, followed by three long, right and left eye-movements. (LEM = Left Eye Movement and REM= Right Eye Movement). Next, the subject mentally estimates a ten-second time interval, again concluding with three eye movements. The lower traces shows eye movements from a dreaming subject counting and estimating time, with nearly identical results. Notice that the EEG traces, though lower in voltage during dreaming, are low and irregular, a typical feature of waking consciousness. EMG is the electromyogram, the electrical activity of muscles, which is known to be suppressed during dreams. Objective evidence for lucid dreaming confirms the hypothesis that dreams involve a conscious state.

helplessly into the persuasive reality of dreams—or of all the other virtual reality states we are attracted to, from drugged states to the persuasive fantasies of true believers everywhere in the world.

Lucid dreaming can be enthralling. Stephen LaBerge has now started an organization for "oneironauts," volunteers who experiment with lucid dreaming in their own nightly lives, regularly sending in dream descriptions. By all accounts it is an enthralling adventure, much safer than other mind-altering methods.

In the late 1940s the American psychiatrist Nathan Rapport wrote about lucid dreams,

As to the mysterious glories all too seldom remembered from dreams—why attempt to describe them? *Those magical fantasies, the weird but lovely gardens, these luminous grandeurs; they are enjoyed only by the dreamer who observes them with active interest, peeping with apprecia-tively wakeful mind, grateful for glories surpassing those the most accom-plished talents can devise in reality.* [quoted in LaBerge, 1985, pp. 40–41]

If you want to experience alternative realities, the ones your brain creates each night may be worth trying.

The Functions of Dreaming and Sleeping

We are abysmally ignorant of the reasons why we dream and sleep. Functional explanations in biology are difficult to prove anyway—they are mostly post hoc, and there is no accepted procedure for proving a functional explanation—and but we do not know of a single persuasive reason for sleep to take up a third of our lives. Sleep makes us vulnera-ble to predators, yet it dates back to the earliest vertebrates. As for dreaming, a hundred years after Freud produced its most popular expla-nations we still have no certainty.

It is normal waking consciousness that is most obviously functional. Without consciousness, all the adaptive advantages we humans pos-sess—language, the ability to learn, intelligence, the use of hands to manipulate the world, socialization, the ability to pass cultural discov-eries to new generations —all of these human advantages would dis-appear. Contrary to widespread belief, normal working consciousness is the most obviously adaptive state of the brain.

Further Reading

J. Allan Hobson, a leading researcher on dreams, has written a fine popular account of the state of scientific understanding in *The Dream-ing Brain*, and Stephen LaBerge's *Lucid Dreaming* (1985) covers that fascinating topic in a highly readable way. Ernest R. Hilgard, one of the most widely respected experimental psychologists, provides a fascinat-ing story of hypnotic effects in *Divided Consciousness: Multiple Con-trols in Human Thought and Action,* (1977), and Matthew Erdelyi has written a sympathetic overview of psychoanalysis from the perspective of cognitive psychology in *Psychoanalysis: Freud's Cognitive Psychology* (1985).

Part III

USING THE THEATER

*O*ur experience in this fleeting instant is deeply shaped by choices we can no longer bring to mind and by intentions now taken for granted. All the conscious moments of the past still haunt the present. Context is, in a way, all our accumulated life knowledge as it shapes and molds our being in the moment. Some contexts are best described as expectations, others as intentions, and some have become a part of our very selves. The following chapters explore these varieties of contextual influence.

BEHIND THE SCENES:
THE CONTEXTS
THAT SHAPE OUR EXPERIENCE

*I*n this book we will use the word *"context"* to describe the great array of unconscious mental sources that shape our conscious experiences and beliefs.

Every visual experience is shaped by contextual assumptions. Because we use reflected light as our main source of visual information, our assumptions about the incoming light shape visual consciousness. A black object can be experienced as bright white, simply by darkening the room and beaming a spotlight at it. But this effect lasts only as long as the spotlight is unconscious—once you notice dust motes dancing in the beam of light, the object turns black again. You can turn impact craters in pictures of the moon into visible bubbles, simply by turning the photograph so that the sunlight seems to come from below. Your visual brain interprets the craters as bubbles because it assumes that all light comes from above, as indeed it does for earth-dwelling creatures. Your sense of space, distance, and size in a room can be profoundly distorted by using trapezoidal walls instead of rectangular ones, again because we have come to expect rooms to have rectangular walls and interpret trapezoidal projections to the eye as rectangles.

Hundreds of mental context effects are known. Even expectations and intentions can be viewed as contexts, since they are largely unconscious in detail but guide conscious experience and voluntary action. "Context" in the sense developed here may be a little bit difficult to understand at first, but once the idea becomes clear, you will see it operating everywhere.

Imagine stepping onto a small sailboat on a fine, breezy day and setting off for a short sail. The weather is fair, and as you set sail from the harbor the water becomes choppy but not uncomfortable. At first, the horizon seems to swing up and down, but you quickly realize that it is the boat that is moving, not the horizon. As you gain your sea legs the world becomes much steadier. On the way home the movements of the boat seem almost placid, though the force of the wind and the waves has not changed. Your sailboat is tied up to the dock, and as you step back on dry land, the horizon suddenly seems to sway, and you must steady yourself; but very quickly the world becomes stable again.

This everyday experience sums up the topic of this chapter. As we walk, dance, run, turn, sit, or climb on dry land, specialized components of the nervous system make running predictions to compensate for our changing relationship to gravity and to the visual surround. The world is experienced as stable only when this remarkable feat of prediction is successful. These orientational predictions are entirely unconscious, but they profoundly influence our conscious experience. As long as they are successful, these contextual predictions give no sign of their existence. That may change for a time when we step on a small sailboat, but in a curious way: We still do not experience the change in the framework of our experience, we just notice an instability in the entire perceptual field. Stepping on the sailboat, we experience the novel, unpredictable movements of our body as a change in the world, even though we know full well that the world has not changed; only our relationship to it has. The real world does not sway with the motion of the deck. The same thing happens for a moment when we step back on dry land after "gaining our sea legs": Unconsciously we now predict a regular yawing and rolling, so that the relationship between reality and expectation has once more gone awry. This experience of an unstable world causes the contextual orientation system to revise its predictions again, and since we are experienced land walkers, we soon regain our feet.

Figure 5-1. *A context effect.* Conscious experiences often evoke *contexts*, unconscious processes that serve to shape later conscious experiences. Once you perceive the hidden figure, you will see it again whenever you look at this picture, for the rest of your life. What has changed in your brain?

The brain system that computes our orientation to gravity and the visual world is part of the mental *context* of our experience. We continually benefit from a host of such mental contexts without experiencing them as objects of conscious experience. Their influence can be inferred from many sources of evidence. The example of the sailing trip involves perceptual-motor context, but much the same argument can be made for the mental contexts for thinking, belief, and communication.

A Demonstration: Creating a New Context

Are you ready to change your brain. . .*forever*? This is not going to hurt. (In fact, you have been doing it all your life.) Take a look at Figure 5-1 and see if you can decide what it shows. It may take a little while—if you must cheat you can hold the page up to the light. Now look at the figure in the normal way. Familiarize yourself with the object in the picture for a minute or so, and forever after in your life you will see it in this new way.

You have just created a mental *context*, simply by becoming conscious of a stimulus and giving your visual system time to adapt to it.

"Context" is a key idea in consciousness studies. It can be defined as any source of knowledge that shapes conscious experiences without itself being conscious. Mental contexts include currently unconscious *expectations* and *intentions*. They are a bit tricky to think about because by definition we do not experience them directly. But contexts are so pervasive that they richly repay the effort to understand.

Here are four pervasive sources of evidence for unconscious contexts that shape conscious experience:

- *Priming* or *context-setting* effects, which show how one conscious experience alters the mental context for future experiences;
- *Fixedness*, where unconscious contextual assumptions stand in the way of solving a problem;
- *Expectations*, which shape our conscious experience of any event that is uncertain;
- *Violations of expectations*, which can cause a part of the unconscious context to become conscious and reportable.

Priming Effects to Set the Scene

When one experience affects the interpretation of another one, we can say that the first event has "primed" or set the mental context for the second event. This is a phenomenon of great generality. Fraisse, for example, writes:

> When I listen to speech, I perceive the clause being pronounced by the speaker, but I interpret it in accordance with all the sentences which I no longer perceive and of which I have only retained a general idea. When I listen to music, I perceive again and again a short, rhythmic structure, but this is integrated with a melodic whole to which it owes its affective resonance. [Fraisse, 1963, p. 46]

In a piece of music the harmonic key and rhythm, the initial statement of the themes, their development and variations all shape the way we experience a single phrase much later, in the middle of a symphony. But none of those initial conditions are conscious when we experience that later phrase.

We can easily show priming in language. Compare these two examples:

pages: book

versus

arrest: book

Your interpretation of "book" will differ depending upon the preceding prime.

The *Oxford English Dictionary* devotes seventy-five thousand words to the many different meanings of the little word "set." It can be a verb, noun, or adjective. It can be a game in tennis or a collection of silverware. We can *set* a value on an antique or look at a stage *set*. Glamorous people make a jet set, and unlucky ones a set of fools. The sun sets, but its location in the sky is certainly not set. Mathematicians use set theory, but psychologists talk about set as readiness to experience something.

Notice how rapidly and smoothly we change our mental set about the word "set." In each use of the word above you had little difficulty understanding the meaning, providing you had sufficient *contextual* information to make it fit. But the detailed process of relating contextual information to your choice of meaning is unconscious. Word ambiguity is one of the most basic and revealing facts of human psychology. Ambiguity is found in all the senses and motor control systems, in thinking and memory, even in feelings. When we take information out of context it generally becomes ambiguous.

Priming effects are ubiquitous in sensation, perception, comprehension, and action. Priming effects are not always momentary; they can last as least as long as a conversation, and in the case of traumatic experiences priming effects can last for years.

Fixedness: Being Blind to "the Obvious"

What do the Charge of the Light Brigade, the Vietnam War, and Figure 5-1 have in common? They all show how unconscious mental set can create a single fixed interpretation of ambiguous information. Mental blind spots like this are universal; we all seem to have them. They are the price we pay for the powerful role of beliefs and expectations in human thought.

The four sentences that follow are normal, coherent English sentences:

1. The ship sailed past the harbor sank.
2. The building blocks the sun shining on the house faded are red.
3. The granite rocks by the seashore with the waves.
4. The cotton clothing is made of grows in Alabama.
   [Milne, 1982, p. 352]

On first reading these sentences, most of us feel "stuck"; they do not cohere, they do not work somehow. We may be driven to try rather far-fetched ideas to make sense of them: Maybe sentence (1) is really two conjoined clauses, such as "The ship sailed past *and* the harbor sank." But harbors do not sink, so that interpretation does not work either. If we truly believe that these are normal English sentences, the experience of trying to understand them can be intensely frustrating and annoying.

What is going on? Consider the following context for sentence (1):

A small part of Napoleon's fleet tried to run the English blockade at the entrance to the harbor. Two ships, a sloop and a frigate, ran straight for the harbor while a third ship tried to sail *past* the harbor in order to draw enemy fire. The ship sailed past the harbor sank.

If you have just encountered sentence (1) for the first time, this little story should help solve the problem. Oh! You mean "The ship (comma) sailed past the harbor (comma) sank !" But that's dirty pool! Not so; the sentence is really quite normal, as we can see when it is put in context.

We could, of course, insert "which" to create:

1. The ship *which* sailed past the harbor sank.

But this use of "which" is optional in English, though we tend to insert it when needed for clarity.

The problem we encountered with sentence (1) is one kind of fixedness. We approach sentences in languages like English with the contextual assumption that the first verb will be the main verb, barring contrary information. If "sailed" is assumed to be the main verb, then we do not know what to do with the verb "sank." But "sailed" may also be the verb of a subordinate clause, as in the following examples:

a. The ship sailed by the commodore was a beautiful sight.
b. The ships sailed at Newport are racing sloops.
c. To my surprise, a ship sailed by a good crew sank .

Here the main verbs always come later in the sentence. The trouble with sentence (1) is that we tend to become committed to one syntactic interpretation before all the evidence is in, and then find it impossible to back away from it. To put it in the most general terms: We are captured by one unconscious interpretation of the beginning of the sentence—we are *fixated* by the wrong syntactic context.

Fixedness can be found in all kinds of problem solving. It is found in vision, language, perception, solving puzzles, science, literature, politics, and warfare. American policy during the Vietnam War may have been an example of fixedness, since it followed certain assumptions about international relations that were widely accepted at the time, across the political spectrum. In retrospect, some of those assumptions may seem questionable. But that is just the point about fixedness: Seen in retrospect or from another perspective, it is hard to believe that a person with fixed beliefs cannot see the "obvious" solution. But within the fixed context the solution is not obvious at all: it is literally impossible to bring to consciousness.

Yet fixedness is a completely normal process. Whenever we try to learn something before we have the knowledge needed to make sense of it, we will are likely to find ourselves interpreting it in the wrong context. The child psycholinguist David McNeill (1966) cites the example of a mother trying to teach her child a sophisticated bit of adult English—a bit prematurely:

CHILD: Nobody don't like me.
MOTHER: No, say, "Nobody likes me."
CHILD: Nobody don't like me.
MOTHER: No, say, "Nobody likes me."
      (Eight repetitions of this dialogue)
MOTHER: No, now listen carefully, say, "Nobody likes me".
CHILD: Oh! Nobody don't likes me.

The trick here is in the linguistic fact that a word like "nobody" has an implicit negation built in, so that a second negative like "don't" is unnecessary. To an adult, "Nobody don't like me" involves a double negative. But that is a sophisticated realization, and it is no wonder that younger children resist it; it seems to violate *their* understanding of syntax. To the child, "don't" is needed because there is no other negation in the sentence. A year later the same child might laugh at the error, but when the dialogue was recorded he or she was not prepared to perceive the difference. In learning, as in life, readiness is all.

A major point here is that our notion of "fixedness" depends critically on seeing the problem from an outside point of view, in which the supposed mistake *is* a mistake. As adults we may find this example comfortably amusing because we know the adult answer. But for the child the error is no error at all. The "flawed" sentence is not experienced as erroneous; in terms of the child's internalized rules, it is quite acceptable.

Intentions and Expectations: Powerful States of No Experience

Social psychologists Richard Nisbett and Timothy Wilson have made the point that reports of mental states can be quite wrong. New Year's resolutions are notorious examples: We solemnly *claim* to have the intention to stop smoking, lose a few pounds, and stop procrastinating. That might last a week or two, only to succumb in the face of a piece of succulent chocolate cake or a craving for cigarettes. Resolutions *sound like* reports of conscious knowledge ("I *know* I'm really going to stop smoking now") and subjectively they may be impossible to distinguish from reports of genuine, controlling intentions. In fact, our inability to accurately report intentions and expectations may simply reflect the fact that they are not qualitatively conscious. Expectations have no color, no texture, no detail that is available to our experience in the way the touch and texture of this page are available to you. Subjective reports of perception, images, inner speech, problem solving, recall, and the like work quite well; but contextual processes seem difficult to report accurately.

William James pointed out in a famous passage on the tip-of-the-tongue experience that waiting for an expected word to arrive is *not a qualitative state*, as you can plainly verify by setting up expectations for a future event that never ———. What is your experience of the missing word before it comes to mind? It certainly seems less specific than a visual image of your front door or the sound of repeating a telephone number in your inner speech.

Intentions and expectations seem to correspond to nothing at all in our experience, but they are very real and powerful in running the brain. The intention to remember a missing word, according to James, involves

> a gap that is intensely active. A sort of a wraith of the name is in it, beckoning us in a given direction, making us at moments tingle with the sense of our closeness, and then letting us sink back without the longed-for term. If wrong names are proposed to us, this singularly definite gap acts immediately so as to negate them. They do not fit into its mold. [James, 1890, p. 245]

Something is going on—we are conscious of some sort of definite state, because if someone suggests the wrong word to us, we know immediately that it is wrong. And we also immediately recognize the right word when it comes to mind. In theoretical terms, we can successfully recognize matches and mismatches of the state of looking for a forgotten word, and the ability to accurately detect matches and mismatches implies that this state involves a *representation* of the target word. Since words can vary along many dimensions, it must be a complex representational state, much like a mental image or a percept. Further, the "tip-of-the-tongue" state takes up the limited capacity associated with consciousness: it excludes other conscious contents. We cannot search for a forgotten word and at the same time contemplate a watercolor, think of yesterday's breakfast, or do anything else that involves conscious experience or mental effort. The intentional state occupies our brain's limited capacity for conscious thought.

But the TOT state does *not* have experienced qualities. Two different TOT states are not experienced as sounding different, even though the words they stand for sound different. The same may be said whenever we intend to speak a thought that is not yet clothed in words. James writes:

> And has the reader never asked himself what kind of a mental fact is his *intention of saying a thing* before he has said it? It is an entirely definite intention, distinct from all other intentions, an absolutely distinct state of consciousness, therefore; and yet how much of it consists of definite sensorial images, either of words or things? Hardly anything! Linger, and the words and things come into the mind; the anticipatory intention, the divination is there no more. But as the words that replace it arrive, it welcomes them successively and calls them right if they agree with it, it rejects them and calls them wrong if they do not. It has therefore a nature of its own of

the most positive sort, and yet what can we say about it without using words that belong to the later mental facts that replace it? The intention *to-say-so-and-so* is the only name it can receive. [1890, p. 245]

James suggested that perhaps one-third of our psychic lives consists of states like this; moreover, he seems to say that this state itself triggers off retrieval processes, which produce the words that will clothe the intention. In other words, the TOT state is active; it initiates a conscious display of a series of candidate words, and "it welcomes them . . . and calls them right if they agree with it, it rejects them and calls them wrong if they do not."

Thus, the TOT state involves a complex representation of the missing word, as shown by the fact that it accurately matches and mismatches candidate words. It competes for the brain's limited capacity system, as do other conscious states; witness the fact that the TOT state excludes other conscious events. It helps trigger word retrieval, so that candidate words come to consciousness as long as the expectation dominates limited capacity. And it stops dominating our minds only when the right word is found or when we give up the search.

In spite of all these properties the TOT state does not have experiential qualities like color, warmth, flavor, location, and intensity. It is therefore radically different from other conscious experiences such as mental images, feelings, inner speech, and percepts.

These observations apply generally to intentions and expectations. To create such experiences for any action, we need only ask someone to get ready to perform the action and then delay the moment of execution. To have a runner experience a "tip-of-the- foot" experience, we need only say "GET READY," "GET SET," and then delay "GO!" At that point the runner is poised to go, the "intention" is at its highest pitch, and yet the action is not executed. There may be no sensory experience of the "intention to run," but the runner's concentration will still be impaired by interfering conscious events. The "intention to run" takes up limited capacity just like the tip-of-the-tongue state does.

We have seen that intentions are complex, nonqualitative contexts, capacity-limiting events, but they are unlike ordinary conscious events in that they are not experienced in detail. To become reportable, intentions must be converted into a qualitative code like inner speech, visual imagery, or perhaps bodily feelings. The TOT state is enormously informative about the contexts that shape our thoughts and actions, however unconsciously they operate.

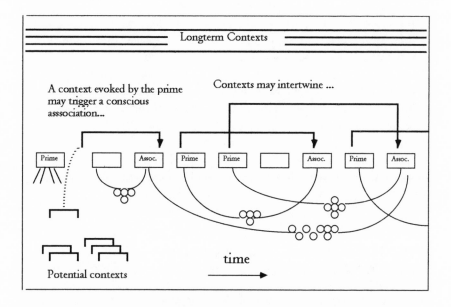

Figure 5-2. *The hidden logic of the stream of thought.* Consciousness often seems to leap from thought to unrelated thought, rarely following an idea to its logical conclusion. How then do we think through a problem in everyday life? This figure shows the stream of consciousness as a set of intertwined problem-solving triads, each one beginning with a conscious prime, which triggers unconscious processing, finally emerging as an associated answer downstream (see Figure 2-2). Many such problem-solving triads may be active at the same time, each one intermittently coming to consciousness. From this point of view, the apparent aimlessness of spontaneous thought may be an illusion; the stream of consciousness is actually driven by many specific purposes, (From Baars, 1988)

The Stream of Consciousness

Figure 5-2 gives us a general way to visualize context effects. Conscious experiences may evoke new contexts: unconscious expectations and goals that can shape later conscious experiences. In a way this fits our previous idea of spontaneous problem-solving, where we ask a conscious question that triggers unconscious problem-solving. The solution may then come to mind spontaneously, without further effort. This is of course the common pattern of memory recall and dozens of other everyday tasks (see Figure 2-3).

In a famous passage, William James remarked that the stream of thought is in constant change.

[L]ike a bird's life, it seems to be made of an alternation of flights and perchings. The rhythm of language expresses this, where every thought is expressed in a sentence, and every sentence closes with a period. The resting-places are usually occupied by sensorial imaginations of some sort. . . . The places of flight are filled with thoughts of relations, static or dynamic, that for the most part obtain between the matters contemplated in the periods of comparative rest. . . . [1890, p. 269]

In our terms, it is the contexts that lead from one conscious event to another. Priming stimuli can evoke existing contexts, as shown in Figure 5-2, or new contexts can be learned from interpreting new experiences, as in the Dallenbach Cow of Figure 5-1.

Breaking Context: Strong Violations May Become Consciously Accessible

While we are usually unaware of their presence, unconscious contexts can become consciously accessible. Every statement we hear or read has presupposed (contextual) information that must be understood before it can make sense. But these contextual presuppositions remain unconscious unless they are violated. This process has been called *decontextualization,* and it is a theoretically central phenomenon. In our chapter on "self" (Chapter 7), we will see how major violations of one's life expectations and intentions can lead to self-alien experiences, from posttraumatic intrusions into the stream of consciousness to the disorders called *depersonalization, fugue,* and *multiple personality disorder*.

Postmodernism is an intellectual movement that deliberately aims to violate our contextual assumptions about gender and social relations in an effort to objectify previously unconscious beliefs. It is the intellectual equivalent of a roller-coaster ride for those with a taste for new and different perspectives. Its pros and cons are hotly debated, but for our purposes "postmodern rhetoric" serves to illustrates both the pervasiveness of unconscious assumptions about such things as gender, and the "objectification" of those assumptions when they are violated.

Damage to Contextual Systems in the Brain

We tend to think that brain damage affects conscious contents, but sometimes the loss seems to be in the *context* of experience. If you touch your head just above your right ear, your finger is only a centimeter away from a part of cortex called the right *parietal lobe*. People

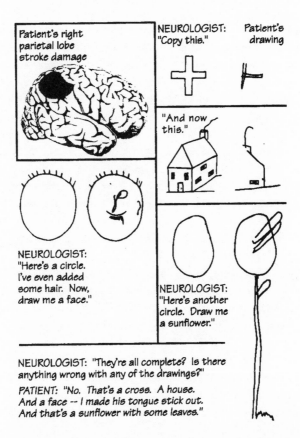

"Neglect" of left side of visual space

Figure 5-3. *Brain damage to a context system.* Neural damage often degrades conscious *contents* in such a way that people can specify what is missing from their normal experience. However, when the right parietal cortex is damaged due to stroke, there is often a loss of ability to experience the left side of visual objects in general. It is a deficiency in the spatial *framework* of visual experience, rather than in specific contents of experience. Such visual neglect seems to involve a loss of *context.* Since context is unconscious, victims cannot specify what is missing, and may engage in bizarre rationalizations, to account for missing information. Damage on the exact opposite side of the brain rarely yields this pattern.

who suffer damage to their right parietal lobes sometimes show *attentional neglect* in the left half of their visual world (see Figure 5-3). They are not blind on the left side of the visual field; rather, they seem to find it impossible somehow to make sense of the left half of visual objects and scenes.

The Italian neurologist Eduardo Bisiach published a famous study some years ago showing that patients with attentional neglect even have visual images in which the left half is degraded and lost. His experiment was performed in Milan, which has a famous square called the Piazza del Duomo, well known to all Milanese. Bisiach asked a woman patient suffering from parietal damage to visualize the Piazza from one side and name all the buildings she could see in her mind's eye. As expected, the patient's buildings were all on the *right* side of her mental image, not on the left. Next he asked her to imagine standing on the *opposite* side of the square, visualize the *same* buildings from that perspective, and name them again. Now the missing buildings could be named. The patient apparently had not lost her memory of the Piazza but was unable to access the left side of her mind's eye from any single point of view.

Note that the brain damage here does not appear as a gap in conscious experience; victims of neglect do not know that they fail to fill in the left side of things. When the retina is damaged severely, a piece of the visual field is lost. Although the brain tries to fill in the missing information, the victim *knows* that something is missing. In the case of parietal neglect that knowledge is unavailable. That may be because the damage is in the *framework* of visual experience, the context and not the contents of consciousness. It is just as if the patient has entered a state of contextual fixedness, and like people living in a world bounded by fixed but unsupported beliefs, they simply do not know, indeed they *cannot* know, that anything is wrong.

Conceptual Contexts

Whatever we believe with absolute certainty we tend to take for granted. More accurately perhaps, we lose sight of the fact that alternatives to our stable assumptions can be entertained. Scientific revolutions can take place when one group of scientists begins to challenge an assumption that is held to be immutable (and hence is largely unconscious) in the thinking of a scientific establishment. Albert Einstein described this phenomenon in nineteenth century physics:

> [A]ll physicists of the last century saw in classical mechanics a firm and final foundation for all physics, yes, indeed, for all natural science. . . . Even Maxwell and H. Hertz, who in retrospect appear as those who demolished the faith in mechanics as the final basis of all physical thinking, *in their conscious thinking* adhered throughout to mechanics as the secured basis of physics. [Einstein, 1949, p. 21; italics added]

Some pages later he recalls how he gained the insight that led to the Special Theory of Relativity:

> After ten years of reflection such a principle resulted from a paradox upon which I had already hit at the age of sixteen: If I pursue a beam of light with the velocity c (the velocity of light in a vacuum), I should observe such a beam of light as a spatially oscillatory electromagnetic field at rest. However, there seems to be no such thing. . . One sees that in this paradox the germ of the special relativity theory is already contained. Today everyone knows, of course, that all attempts to clarify this paradox satisfactorily were condemned to failure as long as the axiom of the absolute character of time, viz., of simultaneity, unrecognizedly was anchored in the unconscious. [p. 25]

Time for a Little Humility

Are we not all imprisoned by our own beliefs? We have treated contexts in this chapter from a God's-eye view, as if we are not ourselves guided by unconscious intentions, expectations, and perceptual assumptions. Not true, of course. All of us walk around with our heads stuck in invisible glass-sided boxes, contextual beliefs and assumptions that frame our choices and perceptions. We need such invisible contexts to operate in the world; there is no such thing as an ultimately decontextualized point of view.

Having said that, I do not believe this humbling reflection necessarily leads to philosophical relativism. Some hypotheses about conscious experience (to take just any topic) are more accurate than others. If our aim is accuracy and inclusiveness, there is such a thing as a more truthful framework, a context that allows us to avoid unnecessary fixedness and to create more encompassing beliefs. That is the role of a useful theory in science.

Further Reading

There are no introductions to the issues of context raised in this chapter, but any book about perception or cognition will cite a number of examples. John Bransford's very readable *Human Cognition* (1979) is excellent, and Michael Polanyi's classic *The Tacit Dimension* (1966) is also a valuable source of examples.

VOLITION:
CONSCIOUS CONTROL OF ACTION

We know what it is to get out of bed on a freezing morning in a room without a fire, and how the very vital principle within us protests against the ordeal. Probably most persons have lain on certain mornings for an hour at a time unable to brace themselves to the resolve. We think how late we shall be, how the duties of the day will suffer; we say, "I must get up, this is ignominious," etc.; but still the warm couch feels too delicious, the cold outside too cruel, and resolution faints away and postpones itself again and again just as it seemed on the verge of bursting the resistance and passing over into the decisive act. . . .

Now how do we ever get up under such circumstances? If I may generalize from my own experience, we more often than not get up without any struggle at all. We suddenly find that we have got up. A fortunate lapse of consciousness occurs; we forget both the warmth and the cold; we fall into some revery connected with the day's life, in the course of which the ideas flashes across us, "Hollo, I must lie here no longer"—an idea which at that lucky instant awakens no contradictory or paralyzing suggestions, and consequently produces immediately its appropriate motor effects. . . .

It was our acute consciousness of both the warmth and the cold during the period of struggle, which paralyzed our activity then and kept our idea of rising in the condition *wish* and not *will*. The moment these inhibitory ideas ceased, the original idea exerted its effects.

This case seems to me to contain in miniature form the data for an entire psychology of volition.
—WILLIAM JAMES, THE PRINCIPLES OF PSYCHOLOGY [ITALICS ADDED]

*I*s "the will" a scientific reality? Using phenomenogical contrasts we can show that two physically identical actions are experienced differently if one is voluntary and the other not. For instance, we can voluntarily imitate an involuntary slip of the tongue, but the imitation is experienced as voluntary, while the slip is not. Likewise, voluntary actions tend to become automatic and free of voluntary control with practice; if we then try to stop or control them, we will experience them as involuntary. In both examples the physical action does not change, but the experience of volition does. Such cases suggest that volition is very real indeed. A body of neurological evidence supports the same conclusion.

William James suggested that an entire theory of voluntary action might be derived from considering the act of rising from one's warm bed on a freezing winter morning. The act of standing up, he thought, occurred spontaneously when a goal image—the thought of standing—came to consciousness long enough to trigger unconscious effectors, the nerve centers that control one's muscles. If the thought of standing up was not inhibited by contrary ideas, such as fear of the cold, it would simply take effect "by default." But as long as a conscious inner debate occurred about the pros and cons of rising, action would be inhibited.

James's *ideomotor theory* fits the theater metaphor of consciousness remarkably well. The theory shows how a conscious goal can recruit and activate automatisms to carry out a voluntary act.

When behaviorists in science and philosophy expelled consciousness about 1900, they also turned away from the two sister issues of voluntary control and self. Even today, discussions of "volition" become entangled with the metaphysical issue of free will, as if the only alternative to an automatic mental process is one that demands the absolute liberty of the soul. In the same way, the common sense idea of "self" is often criticized because it is assumed to lead to unresolvable conceptual paradoxes (Chapter 7).

In this chapter we look at volition, using the same approach that seemed to work for consciousness. That is, we ask, can we find examples of very similar voluntary and nonvoluntary actions that are experienced as profoundly different? Can we find phenomenal contrasts? The answer, as we shall see, is a clear "yes."

How, then, should we characterize the contrasts? It turns out that "voluntary control" is equivalent to "conscious control" (just as common sense suggests) and that a theory proposed by William James about the relationship between conscious goals and voluntary control fits the facts very nicely. The major features of volition emerge when we apply the theater metaphor to action.

Is There a Problem of Volition?

Volition has been neglected as long as consciousness, in part because it has been difficult to show that voluntary control involves a difference that *makes* a difference. Neurologists never dropped volitional terms from their vocabulary. In the brain the differences between voluntary and involuntary functions are simply too marked to be ignored. For example, the Autonomic Nervous System, which controls the smooth muscles of the heart and intestines, is so named because it works "autonomously," outside of voluntary control. External muscles, on the other hand, operate voluntarily: one can be asked to raise an arm but not to change heart rate or intestinal movement. Their neuronal pathways are entirely separate.[1]

Everyone knows the difference between a spontaneous smile and a voluntary one. Spontaneous smiles seem to happen to us; voluntary ones are planned. Paul Ekman is the best-known pioneer in detailed studies of facial expressions and has exhaustively catalogued the muscle movements that make up emotional expressions. Ekman and coworkers consistently find that spontaneous expressions, such as genuine smiles, are visibly different from voluntary ones.

The brain differences between voluntary and spontaneous expressions are also quite clear. Patients with damage to the facial part of the motor cortex cannot smile on request, but they still smile spontaneously. Damage that is limited to areas *below* the cortex can result in just the opposite pattern: Patients can smile on request, but they do not show spontaneous smiles. Thus cortex is needed for voluntary smiles, and subcortex seems to handle spontaneous expressions. It is a clean division of labor.

When the control of facial expressions is impaired by tumor or stroke, a remarkable operation called *facial anastomosis* can sometimes restore normal expressions. In just the way a new branch may be grafted onto the trunk of a tree, the nerves that control facial expressions can be spliced to the brain roots of a neighboring cranial nerve, the spinal accessory nerve. When the procedure is successful the patient recovers voluntary control of facial expressions, but spontaneous expression does not come back, presumably because the subcortical control of the face is still lost. On the other side, in a subcortical disorder called *pseudobulbar palsy,* voluntary facial expressions are lost, but patients continue to show *in*voluntary laughing and weeping. In facial control, therefore, there is a clear and unmistakable contrast between voluntary and spontaneous modes of emotional expression, depending on whether it is initiated cortically or not.

It seems that two identical actions may be psychologically quite distinct, but not because of a difference in complexity, as the early behaviorists thought. Voluntary actions are not just complicated agglomerations of simple reflexes; involuntary components put together do not result in a voluntary act. Something else is involved in volitional control.

William James Getting Out of Bed

We began this chapter with the image of William James on a cold winter morning, reluctantly trying to persuade himself to get out of bed, in a time when heating systems did not automatically turn on in the morning but required shivering minutes to light the fire. For James, this image goes to the very heart of the psychology of volition. He believed that a successful act of will does not typically emerge from some titanic inner struggle. Rather, he claimed, we simply wait until the conscious goal, often an image of the action, can emerge for a while without competing images or intentions. At that moment the action occurs automatically, spontaneously, and without struggle.

James explained conscious control of action by an ideomotor theory in which conscious goal images without effective competition serve to organize and trigger automatically controlled actions, which then run off without further conscious involvement, by default. For James, conscious contents are inherently "impulsive." Of course most of any action is unconscious. The only conscious components of action are:

a. the "idea" or goal (really just an image or idea of the outcome of the action);
b. perhaps some competing goal;
c. the "fiat" (the "go signal", which might simply be release of the inhibitory resistance to the goal); and finally,
d. sensory feedback from the action.

We will see that the theater metaphor invites a natural interpretation of James's ideomotor theory. One use of the theater is to have multiple audience members inspect a single conscious goal and to compete against it if it is found wanting. That is, many audience members may monitor and edit any conscious goal or plan. This is actually the way NASA rocket launches are controlled. Dozens of engineers sit at computer control panels watching the vital signs of the launch—ignition temperature and pressure, signs of leakage and loss of pressure in the coolant, signs of deviation from the set course. Any of these controllers can abort the launch if vital parameters go outside of set boundaries. And of course we can think of the launch parameters as global variables, messages from the actor in the spotlight onstage.

All Actions Have Automatic Components

Most details of routine actions like reading or writing must be automatic: we could never control their numerous details, given the limited capacity of the conscious system. Usually only the novel features of an action are conscious and under voluntary control. But automatic aspects of an act can sometimes become unwanted. This becomes clear when we try to control "bad habits" that have been practiced for years: almost everyone seems to have at least one, whether it is overeating, smoking, nervous gestures, et cetera. These habits are characteristically difficult to control voluntarily; they escape control especially when conscious attention is directed elsewhere.

No doubt unwanted habits have multiple causes, but it is easy to show that sheer automaticity makes it hard to stop an action once its normal triggering conditions are given. As we pointed out above, looking at a word without reading it seems to be quite impossible. The very act of looking at printed words seems to trigger automatisms.

One reason to make goals and plans conscious is that automaticity is a great source of error. The British cognitive psychologist James Reason (1984) has analyzed catastrophic accidents in which fatalities were apparently caused by misplaced automaticity: a London bus driver who crashed a double-decker bus into a low overpass, killing six passengers—perhaps because he was in the habit of driving the same route in a single-decker bus; a train collision killing ninety people because the driver made a habitual turn, but this time onto the wrong track; and the notorious runway collision on the island of Tenerife in 1977, in which a KLM Boeing 747 taxied into the path of a landing jumbo jet, killing 577 passengers and crew. The very senior KLM pilot failed to obtain clearance from the control tower before takeoff, perhaps because he had just finished training hundreds of new pilots in a cockpit simulator, in which runway clearance was not required. In all these cases, Reason suggests that the fatal errors may reflect a "habit intrusion" that is, an inadvertent substitution of a highly automatic action for the correct one.

A similar pattern of accidents may have occurred in flight training with the B-29 bomber in World War II. The B-29 was a four-engine aircraft designed to fly on only one engine in an emergency. As a routine part of flight instruction, three of the four engines were shut off in midflight, to prove to student pilots that the aircraft would indeed continue to fly on just a single engine. For this demonstration to work, the last remaining engine had to be kept running, however, to generate the electrical power needed to restart the others. With all engines turned off, electrical power would be inadequate to restart any engine, and the aircraft would simply lose altitude and crash. Several training flights came to grief when pilots and instructors inadvertently turned the last remaining engine off, rather than turning a second engine on. Turning the last switch "off" may have been an overpracticed automatism. Several of these accidents led to the death of the person making the error —about as strong an argument for the involuntary nature of automatic actions as we might wish to have.

A Loss of Conscious Access Leads to a Loss of Voluntary Control

Ellen Langer of Harvard University and her coworkers have shown that loss of conscious access to an action can cause great problems. One way in which we lose touch with our own competence is by making our skill automatic; when we become skilled readers, musicians, or truck drivers, we lose conscious access to many details of our own actions, and hence become more vulnerable to false evaluations of our own performance. This line of reasoning led Langer to devise a simple coding task that people could learn to the point of automaticity in a matter of minutes. Letters of the alphabet were to be recoded into a two-symbol code; A through J were "a triangle plus the nth letter after A"; K would be "a circle plus the nth letter after J," and so on. Thus the letter "B" would be "triangle plus 2", "L" would be "circle plus 3," et cetera. A preliminary group of subjects reported that they were still conscious of task details after recoding two sentences; after six sentences, they were no longer conscious of the steps. The task had become automatic.

Langer and Imber (1979) now compared the effects of conscious access and automaticity. They devised an arbitrary task in which some of the subjects would be called "Bosses," others were called "Assistants,' and a third group received no label. In fact, the three groups did the identical task; the assumption was that the labels would affect their self-confidence. Afterward they were asked to do the coding task once again. Bosses performed much as before, no different from the no-label group. But Assistants now performed much worse *if* the coding task was automatic; Assistants who were highly automatic in the coding task made four times as many errors as before, and took 40 percent longer to finish. When the coding task was *not* practiced to the point of automacity, Assistants had no problem. They did as well as Bosses.

The simplicity and effectiveness of the Langer and Imber study is quite remarkable. And the interpretation is quite clear: I*if we have no conscious access to our own performance, and if some reliable source of information tells us that we are doing quite badly, we tend to accept misleading feedback because we cannot check our own performance directly.* With direct conscious access to our own performance we are much less influenced by misleading labels. These results suggest that three things go together: consciousness of action details, voluntary control over those details, and the ability to monitor and edit the details. Indeed, the ability to monitor and edit a planned act—to be *responsible* for it —may be the essence of voluntary control.

While we may speak of "conscious" monitoring and editing, the fact is, of course, that we are generally not conscious of the rules and criteria by which we do our monitoring. If we find a syntax error in inner speech, we do not consciously say, "Aha! lack of number agreement between noun and verb!" Rather, we simply "know" immediately that the conscious plan is in error. The rule systems that spot the error are silent in their details. Thus, it is not consciousness that detects errors; rather, conscious experience *facilitates* monitoring by unconscious rule systems, just as the theater architecture facilitates the ability of many audience members to review a global message.

Voluntary Action is Consistent with One's Dominant Goals

Common sense suggests that in voluntary action the goal that is carried out is conscious. Figure 6-1 shows theater diagrams of the ideomotor theory. Notice that saying the sentence "I like ice cream" is constrained by many layers of intentions, some of them purely linguistic, some social and personal, some physical, such as knowing how loudly to speak to be heard in a noisy environment. Most of these contextual factors are unconscious, of course, for any given speech act.

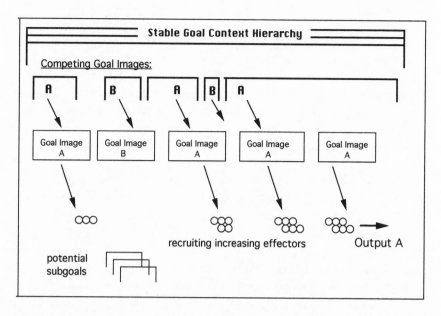

Figure 6-1. *The ideomotor theory of voluntary control.* William James proposed that given enough time in consciousness, mental ideas and images can trigger automatic brain centers that control just the right combination of muscles to carry out specific voluntary actions. Conscious events are only needed to specify the new features of the action in rough terms. Contrary ideas and goals can stop execution, but once goal A gains firm access to the bright spot on stage, the winning goal A is broadcast, so as to recruit and trigger motor control systems that are needed to reach the goal.

The Chevreul Pendulum:
Pitting Visual Images against Intentions

William James proposed that brief conscious goals can trigger complex, unconscious, largely habitual actions. A conscious goal is held to be *in its very nature impulsive*—it tends to be carried out without further ado, barring a competing intention or image.

> A man says to himself, "I must change my shirt," and involuntarily he has taken off his coat, and his fingers are at work in their accustomed manner on his waistcoat-buttons, etc.; or we say, "I must go downstairs," and ere we know it we have risen, walked, and turned the handle of the door;—all through the idea of an end (the image of the goal) coupled with a series of guiding sensations which successively arise. [1890, 1156–57]

A classic demonstration called the Chevreul Pendulum illustrates the ideomotor theory very nicely. It only needs a short piece of string and a small, heavy object for a hanging bob. Hold the string so that the pendulum can swing freely, but *do not move your hands*. It is helpful to prop your elbows on a desk or table to keep your hands still. Now just bring a visual image of the pendulum to mind, swinging in your imagination toward you and away from you, North and South. Try to hold the image for ten or twenty seconds without moving. What do you notice?

Now, without *trying* to move your hands, begin to imagine the pendulum swinging sideways, East and West. What is happening? Most people find that the pendulum begins to swing in whatever direction they imagine it moving, whether North-South or East-West. It seems as if images are more powerful than the intention not to move.

As mentioned in Chapter 3, the word ideo in Greek means "image," and the term "ideomotor" suggests that mental images ultimately control our muscles. If the ideomotor theory is true, there is no mystery to hypnosis and suggestibility: the spectacular performances we see in highly suggestible people simply reflect the centrality of conscious thought in the human brain—the fact that conscious images have widely distributed effects throughout the brain, guiding unconscious centers that control our muscles.

There is a close fit between James's ideomotor theory and the theater architecture. Conscious goals can activate many unconscious action plans and motor routines. If conscious contents are distributed widely among specialized unconscious systems, it makes sense that the goals that need to recruit, organize, and execute action plans and motor routines would need to be conscious. A basic design feature of theater models is that detailed intelligence resides not on stage but in the specialized members of the audience, which can interpret global messages in terms of their local conditions. Once they are settled on, conscious goals tend to execute automatically, barring contrary conscious goals or intentions. Finally, conscious feedback from the results of an action is necessary to correct errors. Consciousness of the error is presumably needed to allow multiple unconscious audience members to organize a better plan for action.

Voluntary Actions Are Shaped by Conscious Feedback

If conscious information is widely distributed, conscious feedback from an action can reveal its success or failure to unconscious planning systems, which may then develop corrective measures. Imagine trying to say "pterosaurus" and actually saying "ptero...ptero...pterosaurus—a momentary stutter that is quite common in speech. Although we have no routine conscious access to the complex articulators and timing systems that control speech, it seems that those specialized systems *do* have access to conscious events. In general, we can learn to avoid errors in the future only if we allow them to become conscious first. Again, unconscious systems seem to be far more subtle and complex and seem to "make use of" conscious information in a distributed sense.

When we become conscious of having made a speech error, we often "repair" it as quickly as possible, but we are never conscious of details of the repair. Many spontaneous speech errors are never repaired, probably because they do not become conscious.

The Netherlands cognitive scientist Willem J. Levelt (1989) has proposed that speech is controlled by listening to oneself—that errors, to be detected and corrected, go through the same auditory and linguistic systems that process normal *perception*. But speech perception is conscious, of course. Feedback from speaking does no good if it is impossible to hear, or if it is masked with noise, or if we are paying attention to something else. Consciousness of errors and the ability to repair them unconsciously seem to go together. It is another example in which consciousness creates effective access to a vast array of unconscious resources.

In sum, James's ideomotor theory can be incorporated straightforwardly into the theater metaphor.

Wanted and Unwanted Automatisms

A skilled typist does not control each finger movement in detail; a skilled reader does not control each eye movement voluntarily; and so on. Automatic processes are part of every voluntary act, and while we cannot control them in detail, they are perceived to be consistent with our goals. We want them.

An army headquarters may set goals for a new direction to march, but thousands of decisions are made locally, without being controlled in detail by the top level of command. Voluntary goals can apparently recruit automatic processes needed to reach the goals. Such automatic routines are then experienced as wanted.

But there are also clearly unwanted actions, such as slips of the tongue. Here, too, there are automatisms at work, but they are out of control, working against one's overall conscious goal. Unwanted actions include slips of speech or action, "bad" habits, and the symptoms of psychopathology.

We can make any automatic component of normal action unwanted simply by resisting it. You can try stopping yourself from reading a word on *this page*, but the very act of looking still triggers automatic reading processes that are not under detailed control. You can try to resist inner speech after looking at a word, or a knee jerk reflex after striking the patellar tendon. The subjective experience of something happening against one's will is very clear.

A Federal Style of Functioning:
Favoring Local Control

Cognitive scientist Peter Greene has maintained for many years that brains have a certain style of functioning which I will call the *federal style*. American readers are familiar with the concept, drawn directly from the ideas that motivated the United States Constitution, a major product of the European Enlightenment, when rationality in human affairs was the great aim. It creates two levels of government. The national government sets policy for the country as a whole, but it is not permitted to exercise power that is not specifically reserved to it. All other powers, in theory at least, are reserved to the States and the people. There is actually a third and fourth level, since towns, villages, and cities in turn are supposed to control local functions that do not strictly require state control, and individuals in their communities are expected to run their own lives as much as possible. The principle is to keep control as close to the people as possible, because it is assumed that local knowledge and enlightened self-interest are superior to centralized control.

It is an interesting idea for running a country that on its founding was the largest democratic nation in the world, orders of magnitude larger and more complex than the countries of Western Europe.

Has the nervous system evolved its own federal style? William James seemed to suggest as much when he wrote, "The study. . .of the distribution of consciousness shows it to be exactly such as we might expect in an organ added for the sake of steering a nervous system grown too complex to regulate itself" (1890, p. 141).

And that is indeed what we have rediscovered in the late twentieth century as a general principle for running extremely complex, distributed systems.

Note

1. There are actually two ways to gain voluntary influence over autonomic functions. Training with conscious biofeedback signals works reasonably well over the short term, but because autonomic systems like the heart, blood vessels, and intestines are controlled by multiple feedback loops, it is difficult to create long-lasting and stable change. The second method is through the use of imagery, where exciting images will tend to arouse the sympathetic (fight or flight) component of the autonomic system, and relaxing images trigger the parasympathetic (rest and recuperation) component. Imagery seems to be the only conscious modality that can trigger autonomic processes.

Further Readings

I do not know of any modern introduction to the psychology of voluntary control. William James's chapters "Will," "Habit," and "Instinct" in *The Principles of Psychology* are still indispensable and fascinating. My *Cognitive Theory of Consciousness* (1988) summarizes much of the modern literature, but it will require a little work. Daniel Wegner's book entitled *White Bears and Other Unwanted Thoughts* (1989) gives a very readable account about some major advances in our understanding of mental control.

THE DIRECTOR:
SELF AS THE UNIFYING
CONTEXT OF CONSCIOUSNESS

The total self (is) partly known and partly knower, partly object and partly subject.... we may call one the Me and the other the I... I shall therefore treat the self as known as the me, and the self as knower, as the I....
WILLIAM JAMES, *PSYCHOLOGY: THE BRIEFER COURSE*

The "self" of everyday life can be seen as a context that maintains long-term stability in our experiences and actions. Over many different situations we still manage to maintain a sense of predictability about who and what we are. A review of "disorders of self" such as multiple personality disorder shows that any fundamental changes in one's expectations and intentions are experienced as self-alien.

Conscious experience invariably seems to involve our *selves. You* are the perceiver, the actor and narrator of your experience, although precisely what that means is an ongoing question. Every statement of personal experience in English refers to a personal pronoun, an *I*, as in "I saw a pussycat," "She believes murder is wrong," and "He smelled a rat." Unconscious and involuntary processes do not mandate a connection with self. "We" do not acknowledge unconscious knowledge as our own, and "we" disavow responsibility for slips and unintentional errors. Yet self is not something we experience directly, as we might experience a musical phrase in a song.

Is this pervasive connection between consciousness and self just an accident of culture, an arbitrary convention? It seems very unlikely, though culture no doubt can modulate the universal theme of self and other. But what exactly does that mean?

The Homunculus and Gilbert Ryle

In 1949, Oxford philosopher Gilbert Ryle famously pointed out a contradiction in the common notion of "the self as observer." He thought it made no sense to postulate an observing self because it does not *explain* anything at all, it merely moves the job of explanation to another level. If we had an observing self contemplating the contents of consciousness, he argued, how would we explain the self itself? By another observer inside the inner self? That would lead to a infinite regress of observing selves each looking into the mind of the preceding one, little imaginary men sitting inside our heads observing each other's observations. The observing self—the *homunculus* or little human—seems to be a fallacy of common sense. Ryle's argument against this "ghost in the machine" has persuaded countless scientists and philosophers that "the self" is a snare and a delusion.

The only trouble with Ryle's impossibility proof is that some notion of self is indispensable and not noticeably problematic in daily life, and indeed in much contemporary psychology. Ryle's impossibility proof applies only if the concept of self is not decomposed into cognitive or brain entities that are better understood than the word "self." As Daniel Dennett has written, "Homunculi are bogeymen only if they duplicate entirely the talents they are rung in to explain. If one can get a team or committee of relatively ignorant, narrow-minded, blind homunculi to produce the intelligent behavior of the whole, this is progress" (1978, p. 123).

William James's "self as agent" must maintain a goal hierarchy distinguishing long-term goals such as survival from momentary goals like reading to the end of this sentence. There may be unsolvable puzzles about self, but there is nothing mysterious about a goal hierarchy. Psychologists like the humanistic theorist Abraham Maslow have long believed that we humans have an ordered series of goals, some more important than others. (see Figure 7-1)

Lovers may risk their lives for loved ones, parents for their children, and combat soldiers for their buddies. Yet even such heroic goals are ordered, one being more important than another. We commonly judge people by the goals that are manifested in their actions. This aspect of "self as agent" does not seem to be impossible to understand.

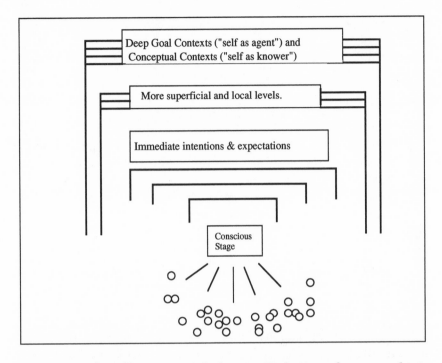

Figure 7-1. *The self as agent and observer.* Violations of our most basic and stable expectations and goals in life are often experienced as invasions of *self.* In that sense, self can be identified with the deepest levels of context: the basic intentions and expectations we have toward the world, ourselves and each other.

Or consider William James's "self as observer." It is hard to see anything impossible about it if we think of observers as *pattern recognizers.* Many brain systems "observe" the output of another, and we now know a great deal about pattern recognizers in the brain for visual, auditory, and conceptual information. Indeed, there seems to be plentiful brain and psychological evidence regarding self-systems.

All that is not to deny the existence of genuine mysteries about self. But it is not all beyond human understanding. If it were, we would have an awfully difficult time dealing with ourselves or other people. As we understand more of the details of the cortical self system, Rylean doubts may begin to sound more and more dated.

Oddly enough, in the sensorimotor area on top of the cortex there are four maps of a little upside-down person, distorted in shape, with every bit of skin and muscle represented in detail. This upside-down map is called the *sensorimotor homunculus,* the little human. The nervous system abounds in such maps, some of which appear to serve as "self-systems," organizing and integrating vast amounts of local bits of information. The anatomy of the brain looks like a physical refutation of Ryle's position.

We will take the notion of an observing and agentive self as useful, as long as the job of explanation is not simply handed on to another level. Any explanation should avoid Ryle's infinite regress. But we must not throw out the baby with the bathwater.

Daniel Dennett has phrased our common intuition about self and consciousness as follows: *That of which I am conscious is that to which I have* access, *or (to put the emphasis where it belongs), that to which I have access. . ."* (1978, p. 151).

"I" have *access* to perception, thought, memory, and body control. Each of us would be mightily surprised if we were unable to gain conscious access to some vivid recent memory, some sight, smell or taste in the surrounding world, or some well-known fact about our own lives, such as our own names. The "self" involved in conscious access is sometimes referred to as the self as observer. William James called it the knower, the "I."

Self as the Overall, Unifying Context of Personal Experience

One way to think of "self" is as a framework that remains largely stable across many different life situations. In theater terms, the implicit self seems to involve the deepest layers of context—the most basic expectations and intentions that guide our lives (see Figure 7.1). Like any context, self seems to be largely unconscious, but it profoundly shapes our conscious thoughts and experiences. It seems to work behind the scenes of the theater, pulling invisible strings to control the spotlight, shaping the actions planned and carried out with the aid of the theater, and to some extent perhaps, the actors themselves.

The evidence for "self as deep context" comes from many sources, but especially from the effects of deep disruptions of life goals. Contexts are after all largely unconscious intentions and expectations that have been stable so long that they have faded into the background of our lives. We take them for granted, just as we take for granted the stability of the ground on which we walk.

It is only when those assumptive entitlements are lost, even for a moment, that the structure of the self seems to come into question. We

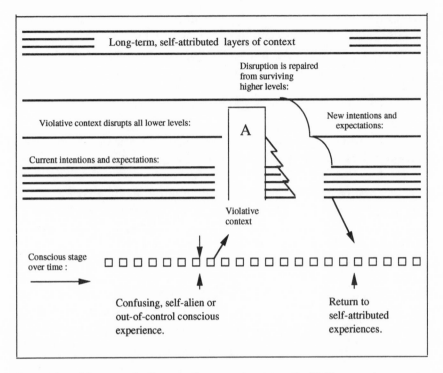

Figure 7-2. *Trauma challenges the organization of self.* Traumatic experiences violate deep levels of expectations and intentions, which are contextual and thus unconscious. As the brain adapts to the violative experience, new levels of context appear.

all know stories about a man or woman losing a beloved friend or spouse, and how such a loss can be experienced as a great gap in oneself. "A part of me seems to be gone" is how a surviving spouse might escribe their experience. In a way, in this chapter we take this common tragedy seriously, as a basic statement about human psychology. Self-relevant events seem to happen at every level of the nervous system see Figure 7-2).

The Sensorimotor Self: Keeping Stability in Body Space

When the eyeball is gently pressed with a finger, the world seems to jump; but as Helmholtz noted in the 1860's, this does not seem to happen with normal eye movements. As you move your eyes across the printed line on this page, your brain must somehow know that it is not the world that is moving, but only the eyes. If the eyes shift ten degrees to the right, our internal map of body space must somehow interpret the shift so as to keep the world stable. But apparently it cannot do so when the eye movement is caused by an outside force. Pushing the eyeball is one of those deceptively simple things that reveals an unsuspected sophistication in the brain. It shows that even for eye movements the brain must know whether it was self- or other-initiated.

This kind of self-other differentiation must occur in any sensor, natural or artificial. If a radar dish rotates at a regular rate and detects an object, it must differentiate between perceived movements due to its own motion and those that are due to movement in the object. Otherwise a building could be interpreted as a rapidly moving object, and a passing flock of birds could be registered as stationary. Self-other differentiation is fundamental for any sensor.

The Narrative Self

At the highest levels of organization we encounter a kind of self that neuroscientist Michael Gazzaniga has dubbed "the interpreter." Unlike the sensorimotor self, the interpreter engages in a narrative, and therefore involves the speaking center of the left hemisphere. What happens when the two hemispheres are severed from each other?

Gazzaniga, who became famous for his studies of split-brain patients, believes that the left hemisphere houses a narrative "interpreter" of experience. He recently wrote,

> We first revealed the interpreter using a simultaneous concept test. The patient is shown two pictures, one exclusively to the left hemisphere and one exclusively to the right, and is asked to choose from an array of pictures placed in full view in front of him the ones associated with the pictures lateralized to the left and right brain.

> In one example of this kind of test, a picture of a chicken claw was flashed to the left hemisphere and a picture of a snow scene to the right hemisphere. Of the array of pictures placed in front of the subject, the obviously correct association is a chicken for a chicken claw and a shovel for the snow scene.

> Split-brain subject P. S. responded by choosing the shovel with the left hand and the chicken with the right. When asked why he chose these items, his left hemisphere replied, "Oh, that's simple. The chicken claw goes with the chicken, and you need a shovel to clean out a chicken

shed." Here, the left brain, observing the left hand's response, interprets that response according to a context consistent with its sphere of knowledge—one that does not include information about the other hemifield snow scene. [1995, p. 1393]

Notice how fluently the narrative self maintains the illusion of its stability in these cases. That is not always true—we will explore the "self-alien" syndromes a little later in this chapter—but different layers of self seem to have a great capacity to simply ignore gaps and discontinuities, up to a point.

When Gaps in the Body Self
Are Filled In by Narrative

Different levels of self seem to work together, so that the narrative interpreter may be able to compensate for even gross violations of the body self. Italian neurologists Eduardo Bisiach and Guliano Geminiani noted this phenomenon with their patients who suffered from neglect of the left side of personal space (see Chapter 5) Neglect is an enigmatic but fascinating disorder, made even more intriguing because it is often accompanied by *anosognosia* (not-knowing). Patients with neglect deny some aspects of their disorder with astonishing tenacity.

Here is a case of a sixty-five-year old woman with a right-hemisphere stroke that paralyzed her left side.

> Alert and cooperative, she claimed that the reason for her hospitalization was a sudden weakness and annoying burning or itching in her right limbs. . . . She also claimed that her left hand did not belong to her but had been forgotten in the ambulance by another patient. On request, she admitted without hesitation that her left shoulder was part of her body and *inferentially* came to the same conclusion as regards her left arm and elbow. . . [Bisiach & Geminiani, 1991, pp. 32–33]

Patients like this often have no loss of intelligence, believing in general pretty much what most people do about their bodies. A frequent feature is a remarkable inventiveness and flexibility in maintaining beliefs about their paralyzed side that are plainly untrue. A sense of alienness about paralyzed limbs is common; the paralyzed limb is sometimes attributed to another person (often a member of the family), or at least not to oneself. Some patients show a fierce hatred toward their alien limbs and may attempt to harm them, occasionally trying to throw their paralyzed arms or legs out of the bed.

Another victim of right-hemisphere stroke cited by Bisiach and Geminiani:

> refused to admit that his left arm belonged to him, unshakenly maintaining that it was the examiner's arm. Because he was an educated man, he could maintain relatively fluent conversations on a variety of topics without disclosing any sign of intellectual impairment. . . . On one occasion the examiner placed the patient's left hand on the bedclothes, between his own hands and asked the patient whose hands they were: Unhesitatingly he replied that they were the examiner's hands. Questioned as to whether he had ever met a three-handed man, the patient, pointing to the three arms in front of him, answered that because the examiner had three arms he must also have three hands. [1991, p. 34]

Such neurological cases are not rare. They show the desperate creativity with which humans maintain as much coherence and stability in their conscious experience as they can, even when the brain itself has gone awry.

And yet, there are some very common cases where the sense of narrative coherence is not maintained. These are "loss of self" or "self-alien" syndromes. Some of this may be experienced when we break a leg, as Oliver Sacks has so beautifully shown in his book *A Leg to Stand On*; some of it may follow a disastrous love affair, a lost job, or a traumatic invasion of the invisible but firm boundaries we all maintain in the world around us—boundaries of body space, social status, privacy, and accepted strength or capability.

A Loss of Self: Depersonalization

The most common self-alien syndrome along these lines, one that is reported by a *majority* of people in late adolescence or early adulthood, is depersonalization, or loss of the sense of who we are. Depersonalization disorder is described as

> an alteration in the perception and experience of the self so that the usual sense of one's own reality is temporarily lost or changed. This is manifested by a sensation of self-estrangement or unreality, which may include the feeling that one's extremities have changed in size, or the experience of seeming to perceive oneself from a distance.. . . the indi-

vidual may feel "mechanical" or as though in a dream. Various types of sensory anesthesias and a feeling of not being in complete control of one's actions, including speech, are often present. All of these feelings are ego-dystonic (self-alien). . . . [Spitzer; 1979; p. 259]

Mild depersonalization is astonishingly common: it is estimated to occur at some time in 30 to 70 percent of young adults.

If self is the overall context of experience, disturbances in self might emerge from violations of context. Depersonalization certainly seems to fit that description. First, it is often triggered by severe violations of everyday expectations about the world, such as military combat or an auto accident, physical pain, anxiety, and depression. It can occur after brainwashing, thought reform, and indoctrination while the captive of cults or terrorists—all cases in which routine, dominant goals and perspectives are profoundly challenged. These facts are consistent with the notion that disruption of the self involves deep context-violation.

The high rate of depersonalization in late adolescence is significant. Most people establish their fundamental goals and expectations during this period in their lives, and many things can challenge any new, tentative integration. If a college student falls in love, a breakdown in expectations about love can create a deep violation of self-as-context.

People suffering from depersonalization sometimes experience others as well in profoundly changed ways. The whole world may seem unreal. The psychiatric manual states that

> derealization is frequently present. This is manifested in a strange alteration in the perception of one's surroundings so that a sense of the reality of the external world is lost. A perceived change in the size or shape of objects in the external world is common. People may be perceived as dead or mechanical. . . . Other associated features include . . . a disturbance in the subjective sense of time." [Spitzer, 1979, p. 259]

As the self is challenged the perceived world may also become estranged.

Remembering Who We Are

Fugue provides another example of a self-alien syndrome. It involves "sudden, unexpected travel away from home or customary work locale with assumption of a new identity and an inability to recall one's previous identity. Perplexity and disorientation may occur. Following recovery, there is no recollection of events that took place during the fugue." (Spitzer, 1979, p. 256). Fugue—which means "flight"—typically "follows severe psychosocial stress, such as marital quarrels, personal rejections, military conflict, or natural disaster." It seems to be related to *psychological amnesia*, in which a loss of memory occurs after severe stress.

Multiple Selves

The most famous example of a self-altering disorder is multiple personality. Scientists have been skeptical about the existence of a multiple-personality syndrome. It is clear, for example, that even experts on the subject find it difficult to distinguish between the true syndrome and determined faking by someone with enough incentive to do so, such as the "Hillside Strangler" in Los Angeles, who used the insanity defense, claiming he was suffering from multiple-personality disorder. But in that respect, multiple personality is not different from a hundred physical disorders, such as back injury, that can also be faked in a hard-to-detect fashion. Yet no one doubts that some people do have genuine back pain, which may be difficult to distinguish from bogus pain in people who are highly motivated to fake the problem.

Researchers in the field came to a working consensus about the reality of multiple-personality syndrome after publication in 1983 of a massively detailed study led by Frank W. Putnam of the National Institutes of Mental Health in the United States. Putnam's work has persuaded knowledgeable skeptics by sheer weight of evidence, based on more than one hundred cases that follow the same extraordinary pattern so consistently that there could hardly be a matter of chance among the patients. Here is a psychiatric description:

> The essential feature is the existence within the individual of two or more distinct personalities, each of which is dominant at a particular time. Each personality is a fully integrated and complex unit with unique memories, behavior patterns, and social relationships that determine the nature of the individual's acts when that person is predominant. . . . Studies have demonstrated that different personalities may have different responses to physiological and psychological measurements. One or more subpersonalities may report being of the opposite sex, of a different race or age, or from a different family than the original personality. . . . The original personality and all of the subpersonalities are aware of lost periods of time. . . . [Spitzer, 1979, p. 257]

Notice that eclipsed personalities report a gap in the flow of experience, just as do victims of amnesia and fugue. The cases studied in recent years reveal not just a few but a dozen or more "alters"—subpersonalities with claims of distinctive perspectives and experiences. Nearly all cases involve long-term physical and sexual abuse in childhood, and the most childlike "alters" seem to hold the "secret" of the abuse. More mature, competent, and adult personalities do not know about the trauma. It seems very unlikely that so many different people, in different places and times, examined in great detail by different observers, would emerge with such a rigid and homogeneous pattern of behavior and experience.

The dozen or more alters in a typical multiple personality case often form a highly predictable group, with one or two adult selves, "hosts," who know about the other members of the group, and who often soothe and reassure the more childlike selves. Alters often know about each other, but their knowledge may be asymmetrical—Joe the adult might know about Johnny the little boy, but not vice versa. Subselves may hear each other or speak to each other, but often with a sense that the voice heard is self-alien, not-self. To the speaking alter, of course, that voice is an essential part of self.

Once again, there is a consistent pattern of evidence that a deep challenge to the normal unifying context may evoke a shift in self. It is reported that "transition from one personality to another is sudden and often associated with psychosocial stress." Obviously, this is consistent with the finding that multiple personality syndrome is almost always associated with a history of severe traumatic abuse in childhood. Psychiatric researchers David Spiegel and Frank Putnam speculate that abused children learn to enter a *dissociated* state of mind, which develops over time into an complete, differentiated self. According to the distinguished experimentalist Ernest R. Hilgard, such deep dissociations can be demonstrated to occur in "hypnotic virtuosos," people who are in the top 1 percent of the general population in hypnotic ability. In the theater framework we can say that separate, deep contexts can emerge in such individuals, and that perhaps, under circumstances of repeated traumatic stress, it could develop in all of us over time.

What Can We Say about Self and Consciousness?

The observing self has routine access to all sensory modalities, immediate memory, recent autobiographical memories, routine personal facts, personal "marker" memories, and future plans or fantasied images. In addition, we have indirect voluntary access to a host of specialized skills that are not conscious, but whose unexpected absence would create great conscious surprise. This is of course the point Daniel Dennett remarked upon in the passage quoted earlier in this chapter, the notion that *self is that which has access to consciousness.*

A rapid change in the access conditions of any of these domains may be perceived as self-alien. Thus loss of expected memories may impact one's sense of self, as would sudden blindness or even a sudden *increase* in one's ability to imagine things. Any rapid change violates contextual predictability, but changes consistent with one's goals should be relatively more acceptable.

The same point applies to action. We expect voluntary control over our external muscles; over mental functions like the ability to recall this morning's breakfast or the ability to express our thoughts; over many objects in our environment; over people, to some extent; and, within limits, over social circumstances. A loss in any area of expected control may be perceived as a profound change in self.

There seems to be a basic connection between self and conscious experience. They are not the same thing but stand in the relation of context to content. The evidence from psychological disturbances of self supports this assumption quite well. The director backstage involves a set of deep layers of expectations and intentions about the world. Being robbed of our ability to have control over our bodies or mental processes, or our social realm, seems to induce a sense, not just of sadness, but of disorientation and otherness, a loss of a piece of ourselves. "Self as deep context" seems to be a useful extension of the theater metaphor.

Further Reading

The literature on "self," in all its aspects, is often technical and rather confusing. It contains important ideas from phenomenology, psychoanalysis, and classical philosophy. A reading of the classic works is very useful. I recommend Anna Freud's *Ego and the Mechanisms of Defense* (1946). Oliver Sacks's *A Leg to Stand On* (1984) is an extended meditation on voluntary control and self.

CONCLUDING THOUGHTS

WHAT IS IT GOOD FOR?
THE FUNCTIONS OF CONSCIOUSNESS

The particulars of the distribution of consciousness, so far as we
know them, point to its being efficacious. . . .
—WILLIAM JAMES, *THE PRINCIPLES OF PSYCHOLOGY*

Consciousness is a supremely functional adaptation. Like other
major biological adaptations it seems to have many uses. The
bloodstream brings vital nutrients to all cells in the body, carries away waste products, transports hormones and immune cells, and
helps to regulate body temperature. Consciousness also has as many
functions, perhaps as many as theaters do. We explore a tentative list
here.

This book always refers to your personal experience as a key source of
evidence, and there is no reason to abandon that now. Just to make
the likely functions of consciousness stand out clearly, consider what
would happen *at this very moment* if you were accosted by some large,
aggressive, and dangerous beast, such as a full-sized angry bullock.
How would you cope? And how would you use consciousness, as
such, to survive, eventually to pass on your genes? That is after all
the criterion for biological adaptations.

   Let us suppose, therefore, that even as you are quietly reading this
sentence you become aware of a strange, fetid, animal odor in the air;
something bovine, a hint of hot moist breath, a restless stamping and

scraping of heavy hooves, a sudden forceful heavy breath of air down your neck. You are naturally reluctant to stop reading, but suddenly a wild thought whether there could be a large animal in the room, breaks through. Something *really* large, like a Saint Bernard dog? A nutty thought, of course, but you find yourself turning your head. . .and as you turn, you discover yourself looking eye to eye about six inches away into the great moist brown eyes not of a friendly big dog but of an immense dark cow, it seems, with a hairy brown face and unbelievably large horns, now tossing ominously in your direction. Without even thinking, you leap from your comfortable chair, and confront the beast from the opposite side of the room. It's not a cow at all, but a great big hairy *bull*, an awesome animal, about the size of a small truck, it seems at first, exuding a nasty rank smell and now beginning to grunt at you in an angry, exasperated way.

It's a do-or-die situation, obviously. Not the sort of thing we encounter on a regular basis in our well-protected world but definitely a problem; in fact, one that is not unlike the daily difficulties confronting our biological ancestors who, over millions of years of evolution, bequeathed to us our ability to be conscious of dangerous animals. There's nothing sophisticated about it; you just hope that your brain is equipped to help you cope.

The Prioritizing Function

Some things are more important than others. In alerting you to danger, your attentional system has already acted. It seems that high-priority stimuli, like the sound of one's own name, are detected unconsciously and then may break through to consciousness.

The prospect of hanging concentrates the mind wonderfully, as Dr. Johnson said, but he probably did not worry much *how* that could be so. We can relate goals such as survival or pleasure to whatever becomes conscious. In putting as much distance as possible between yourself and a raging bull, you surely do not spend much time reflecting on your goal of surviving. Yet your desire to stay alive surely influenced attentional processes unconsciously.

In practice we know very well that a conscious connection is needed to create new priorities. To convince children that smoking is dangerous, we are always trying to make the reality of long-term disaster as vivid and immediate as possible. Consciousness is needed to make the association between smoking and cancer, or other new association. People routinely try to change each other's behavior by associating the change with high-priority goals. It seems that consciousness is needed to change behavior and reorganize priorities.

Problem-Solving Functions

Consciousness creates access to unconscious resources. The act of becoming conscious of a charging bull evokes a host of unconscious processes—those that allow you to run without having to think, routines that search for the right words to yell for help, and some that bring in knowledge from potentially anywhere in the brain to help make sense of it all. Consciousness acts as the gateway to all these sources of unconscious knowledge. It creates access to working memory, to the choices for action, to knowledge sources like the lexicon and semantic memory, and to a vast variety of automatic routines.

We are curious, searching beings because our brain, in its hunger for new information, can create new connections and new integrations between existing islands of knowledge. But such novel connections always seem to require explicit awareness of the new connections.

Consciousness Facilitates Decision Making and Executive Control...but It Takes Time To Do So

If you only had time to *think* while running from the charging bull, you would no doubt be able to come up with some good ideas. Should you wave a red cape at it? Make soothing noises, or try to make friends with it? Try to feed it, stare it down in a contest of wills, or make yourself look as small and humble as possible? Or just run for your life?

The trouble is of course that you have no time to think. Unless you have habitual routines for dealing with charging bovines, you are fated to use whatever unconscious skills you might have learned from dodging traffic and the like. But automobiles do not become enraged and try to follow you up the sidewalk. Your existing routines seem woefully inadequate. Worse, if you start to panic, your conscious limited capacity will be taken up with task-irrelevant thoughts. Don't panic. Use your limited capacity to solve the problem.

If you had a little bit more time you would be able to use one of the most fundamental functions of human experience, as follows.

Consciousness Serves to Optimize the Trade-off between Organization and Flexibility

Automatic, "canned" responses are highly adaptive in predictable situations. When you have time and leisure to think about the problem of the charging bull, you will no doubt be able to think of half a dozen solutions. In the face of novelty and uncertainty, the capacity of consciousness to recruit and reconfigure specialized knowledge sources becomes vital. Given no time and great urgency, however, you can only use prepared actions. It's a fundamental dilemma.

The Ideomotor Hypothesis: Consciousness Helps to Recruit and Control Actions

Madly dodging a dangerous animal may not give you enough leisure to appreciate how well your brain is responding to the next thrust of an angry pair of horns. Nevertheless, chances are that brief conscious thoughts such as "Oh my God! He's coming this way!" serve to mobilize autonomic arousal, rapid muscular responses, and desperate gambits such as throwing pencils and books at the charging beast.

Conscious goals serve to mobilize automatic routines and body muscles in order to organize and carry out voluntary actions. The most spectacular examples involve such things as biofeedback control of alpha waves and single neurons. People can learn this sort of thing with great ease and rapidity, and consciousness of the desired outcome is a necessary condition for this kind of learning to occur.

Consciousness Is Needed for Error Detection and Editing of Action Plans

Now suppose you decide to assert yourself against what is after all a dumb animal; seems like a good idea, right? You climb on top of a chair and tower over the beast, look at it eye to eye, and yell at it. Fortunately, conscious goals and actions are monitored by unconscious systems that act to interrupt execution if errors are detected. Yelling at an agitated bull is an error, as you realize when you leap aside in the nick of time, just as the chair on which you were standing is shattered to pieces. It's a big help to detect errors quickly.

Of course, while we often become aware of making an error in a general way, the details of what makes an error an error are almost always unconscious. You can detect mistakes in the syntax of a sentence without knowing anything about nouns, verbs, prepositions, deep structure, or the other technical complexities of grammar. Your working knowledge of language is far greater than the best of our current theories, but it is unconscious. To gain access to that unconscious knowledge, you need only to be conscious of the target words and sentences. Your brain will tell you when an error occurs, but not why it is an error.

A Gateway to the Self

Having one's personal space invaded by charging bulls is an experience that involves the self as observer, agent, and guardian of the continuity of experience. When a major earthquake in the area of Loma Prieta struck northern California several years ago, researchers were quick to interview students at Stanford University, not many miles away from the epicenter of the quake. Psychiatric investigators David Spiegel and Etzel Cardena learned to their surprise that some 40 percent of Stanford graduate students reported having *out-of-body experiences* during the quake—visualizing themselves in a detached way, as if from the outside, while their bookcases came tumbling down around their heads.

Obviously one major function of consciousness is *to create access for the self in all its manifestations.*Consciousness is, in Daniel Dennett's words, "that. . .to which *I* have access" (1978, p. 151). Conscious experience seems to be the faculty by which the self gains access to the world.

In sudden traumatic experiences people report a wide variety of *dissociative* experiences, altered states of consciousness that have the effect of creating psychological distance from the experience. Even after minor automobile accidents many people report a passing feeling of unreality. Such sudden changes can impact one's sense of self as well as subtle aspects of conscious experience. There are close, reciprocal bonds between self and consciousness.

Consciousness Is Involved in Learning and Adaptation

All this makes sense if we consider that *consciousness is a major factor in adapting to change.* There is a long and still unresolved controversy whether learning can occur without consciousness, a notoriously difficult question to decide. But there is a much easier question: *Is there a positive correlation between consciousness and learning? Do we need more conscious exposure to learn more?* To learn two chapters of that difficult book, do we need twice as much time paying attention to it? The answer is an obvious and resounding yes.

Accommodating to change can take much conscious thought, and indeed, there are life changes to which we never fully adapt. For unwanted changes, roughly speaking, the greater the life change, the longer people are likely to report intrusive experiences—sudden thoughts about the traumatic event, unexpected waves of feelings of distress, and other breakthroughs into consciousness of unwanted sequelae of the trauma.

Can you learn to live with a nasty bovine? The more novelty the brain must adapt to, the longer conscious involvement is needed for successful learning and problem solving. Traditionally in psychology this is called the "law of practice," but it is rarely emphasized that "practice" always means *conscious* practice. Perhaps the behavioristic law of practice should be called "the law of conscious attention." At an everyday level this simply comes down to the obvious point that in order to learn something, we have to pay attention to it. But of course, "paying attention" means that we stay conscious of something. Once we make that translation, the close relationship between learning and consciousness emerges as something we have known for decades.

Consciousness Is Needed to Create the Context for Understanding Any Event

How did the bull get in here? Who could have let it in? Why, in a city where the only wild bulls are in the zoo, is one's room invaded by a great monstrous ox? Why did you deserve to have this bizarre practical joke played on you? These questions may seem to be less pressing than sheer survival, but they are precisely the things that concern people most after any shocking event. After sudden changes we must try again to make sense of the world.

The Access Function of Consciousness

Notice how many functions of consciousness create new kinds of access between otherwise separate domains of knowledge. Indeed, all the functions listed in this chapter involve novel access. The prioritizing function indicates that sources that are more important will come to the conscious bright spot onstage more easily and more often, thereby allowing increased access to the audience and to contextual operators behind the scenes. The ideomotor hypothesis describes how such increased access may be used to control voluntary action.

It seems that the single most prominent function of consciousness is to increase access between otherwise separate sources of informa-

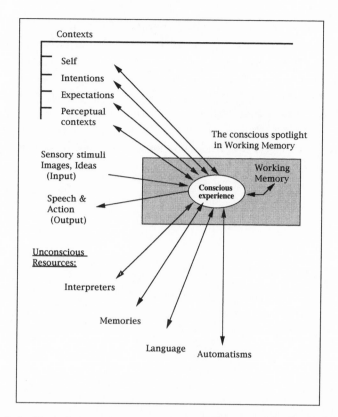

Figure 8-1. *Consciousness creates access.* **Like major biological adaptations, consciousness serves multiple functions. The most important may be called the access function: to facilitate the flow of information between different elements of the mental theater. All of the psychological demonstrations in this book illustrate the role of consciousness in creating novel access.**

tion. Figure 8-1 shows one way to conceptualize this universal access function. Specific examples of the access function, are provided throughout the previous chapters.

Everything in this figure is connected to everything else, via the bright spot onstage; that may seem to be a problem because it threatens to reduce our carefully evolved framework into an undifferentiated theoretical soup. But each element in Figure. 8-1 can be defined operationally, in terms of distinct observable events. These elements are usually separate from each other. Further, many elements such as "self," "working memory," and "sensory input" also have routine interactions that are unconscious and therefore quite fixed. While every-thing in Figure 8-1 *can* interact with everything else, it cannot do so with infinite flexibility.

To allow such universal access we need that little bright spot onstage. But the bright spot of consciousness does not have very fast throughput. It creates a bottleneck that slows thing down. It is, in turn, influenced by the attentional network and other mechanisms.

Is consciousness a functional adaptation? Does it help us to survive? You, the reader, now have all the evidence at your fingertips. What do you think?

EPILOGUE:
A TINY BIT OF PHILOSOPHY

To the reader who has come this far on our shared journey, I want to express my warm gratitude. For the author this book represents a progress report on a project of almost twenty years' time, and one that has provided much satisfaction as well as a fair number of challenges.

There is no doubt in my mind that we have learned a great deal in twenty years. Today, far more scientists than ever before are seeing the issue as open to exploration. Our basis in evidence has grown to formidable size, and theory is more precise and inclusive than ever. To be sure, there are puzzles and paradoxes galore, and there is no guarantee that we can solve them. But my sense, which I hope you share, is that we are making gradual progress toward understanding.

Some scholars still maintain that empirically based understanding of human experience is impossible, or that consciousness simply has no causal role to play in the nervous system. The evidence discussed in these pages suggests otherwise.

Is consciousness a working, biological adaptation? A hundred years ago, in his magisterial *Principles of Psychology*, William James quoted Thomas Henry Huxley—known as "Darwin's Bulldog" for his fierce public advocacy of evolutionary theory—on the role of consciousness. Huxley could not think of any biological function that could be served by our personal experience, and suggested famously that,

> consciousness. . . would appear to be related to the mechanism of the body simply as a collateral product of its working, and to be completely without any power of modifying that working, as the steam-whistle which accompanies the work of a locomotive is without influence upon its machinery. [1890, p. 135]

Huxley was one of the first to say what became a commonplace in twentieth-century behaviorism—that consciousness is a fiction and is of no use at all. It is a claim that simply does not stand up in the face of a flood of evidence. Many basic kinds of informational access are provided by consciousness, and apparently by consciousness alone. These forms of access are systematically and predictably degraded when normal consciousness is lost through stupor, habituation, automaticity, distraction, brain damage, or any other factor. It is something we all know on a daily basis when we urge children to *pay attention* before crossing the street, or when we spend hours *thinking* (consciously) about some difficult problem. Fire engines are painted red and come equipped with sirens to draw the consciousness of drivers and pedestrians in busy traffic. Our daily world runs on the unstated assumption that we must reach the consciousness of other people in order to persuade them of the justice and truth of whatever we believe. We pay attention to things we need to learn, thereby becoming conscious of them. In ordinary life we all act as if our conscious experiences are functional. But for a hundred years, formal science and philosophy have been curiously divorced from this daily reality.

Consciousness appears to be the major adaptive faculty of the brain. Our personal experience of the world is the subjective aspect of that adaptive activity. Philosophical arguments *against* the adaptive function of awareness rely on a little verbal magic, in which we pretend to suck out all of the real features of consciousness—usually the ones that happen to be externally observable today—and ask, is anything left after we take away everything, except the last residuum of subjectivity?

It is a questionable sort of logic. Suppose we apply it to our understanding of mountains. Take the craggy Matterhorn in Switzerland and pretend that we can carve away its northern face, digging deeper and deeper into the heart of the mountain until all the rock has been carted away. Would the southern face of the Matterhorn still exist? It is not a question that makes sense, because mountains are not the sort of things that can be dug out without taking away all of their different sides in the process. Yet that same logic is presumed to apply to other things, like human consciousness. The entire paradox of the mind-body problem seems to rest on an implicit metaphor in which the southern face of the Matterhorn can be separated from the mountain itself. Like a mountain, consciousness may just not be the kind of thing that can be robbed of its publically observable face without taking away its privately observable one.

It is difficult to avoid the conclusion that a century of philosophical physicalism has led us astray, far away from the genuine scientific questions. We have allowed a little word magic, a few conceptual conundrums, to stand in the way of straightforward exploration of the most humanly important topic in the world.

That is not the way good science is done. In the long history of the sciences, it is vital to remember that *conceptual puzzles are the rule whenever we encounter truly new territory, not the exception.* Gravity was a great philosophical paradox in 1650, the roundness of the earth was conceptually bizarre in 1400, and in 1900 space flight was inconceivable to some of the foremost physicists in the world. Historically we do not allow the appearance of paradox to stand in the way of a sensible study of the evidence. Good science requires two legs, the leg of thinking and the leg of evidence. In consciousness studies, we have tried all too often to walk on one leg alone. It is not a good idea.

Compared to Huxley, Charles Darwin himself was much more of a field naturalist, intrigued with real questions regardless of their philosophical inconvenience. In his *Old and Useless Notes* he noted simply that "consciousness seems to be the effect of complexity of [biological] organization" (c. 1838). And indeed it does. That is a scientist speaking, with enough faith to expect conceptual paradoxes to resolve eventually, given the necessary evidence and thought. Darwin's example is the one we should follow today.

MAKE YOUR OWN THEORY:
A SUMMARY OF THE EVIDENCE

*T*his section provides a more technical summary of the major bodies of evidence about conscious experience. By comparing contrasting pairs of phenomena that are very similar except that one is conscious while the other is not, we can hone in on just those elements that are uniquely associated with consciousness. Here are pairs of "conscious versus unconscious" facts that any complete theory must explain. Try to see if you can account for them—with a theater metaphor or in any other way!

Conscious and Unconscious Aspects of Input Processes

There is little disagreement that "perception" is conscious input representation. Even a radical behaviorist like B. F. Skinner suggested that consciousness is associated with "stimulus control." But not all kinds of stimulus representation are conscious. There are at least six categories of comparable *un*conscious stimulus-representation. We will take them in turn.

Below-Threshold or Masked Stimulation

One obvious case where we lose a stimulus from consciousness involves a decrease in the intensity or duration of a stimulus, or masking of one by another. There is a vast literature on subliminal effects produced in this way, revived in 1983 by Anthony Marcel's classic experiments showing that a masked unconscious word, which could not be reported, would still "prime" the processing of a semantically related word. This persuaded many psychologists that unconscious words were still semantically represented in some sense.

Preperceptual Processes

There are several sources of evidence for the view that preperceptual processes are representational. Perhaps the most persuasive involve brain electrical activity evoked by stimuli during coma or deep sleep. Likewise, most words in the language have multiple meanings that do not become conscious in the course of normal language comprehension, so that any ambiguities must be resolved prior to the moment of conscious comprehension. Plentiful evidence suggests that local ambiguities must be resolved with reference to a larger framework representing the visual scene or the linguistic message as a whole. This, too, suggests the need for unconscious preperceptual hypothesis testing before one can arrive at a coherent, conscious representation of the world.

When a stimulus is degraded so that automatic prepercepual processing is blocked, subjects often begin to perform conscious hypothesis-testing. A good example of this occurs in reading upside down, where the letter features and possible meanings of words begin to be tested quite consciously. This appears to be a conscious analogue of a process that normally takes place quickly, automatically, and unconsciously.

Postperceptual Representations

Is a habituated stimulus still represented? The feeling of the chair once we have been sitting for a while, the ambient light and noise level, one's orientation to gravity, and indeed all the multifarious sources of consistent and predictable stimulation in the environment tend to be unconscious. Nevertheless, many students of the subject believe, at least since the work of E. N. Sokolov, that the nervous system continues to represent habituated stimulus events even after they have become unconscious. Sokolov's well-known arguments are based upon the occurrence of an Orienting Response (OR) whenever people or animals are confronted with a novel stimulus. The OR consists of a large set of central and peripheral physiological events, from receptor orientation to blocking of alpha waves, characteristic parts of the evoked potential, and changes in a wide variety of autonomic responses such as increases in sweating, heart rate, capillary expansion or contraction, et cetera. An animal or human being looks for the source of stimulation once a stimulus elicits an OR, so we can be pretty sure that those stimuli are conscious.

Suppose we present people with a train of white noise bursts of a certain duration, spectral distribution, onset and offset slopes, location in space, interstimulus interval, and so on. If the stimulus is not painfully loud, people will lose awareness of it rather quickly, but they will tend to become conscious of the noise again as soon as any stimulus-parameter changes: The noise can become louder or softer, the time between the noise bursts can change, the intensity envelope or the frequency distribution can change—any of these changes will trigger a new OR. To explain this, Sokolov argues, we can only assume that there is a "model of the stimulus" against which the unconscious stimulus is matched; as long as the match fits reasonably well, one does not become conscious of the noise; only when there is a mismatch in any parameter of the stimulus do humans and animals produce another OR. This suggests that all constant or predictable sources of stimulation continue to be represented in the nervous system, even though they are unconscious. Habituated material includes all the things we take for granted, everything that has become predictable.

In sum, it seems safe to conclude that postperceptual (habituated) stimulus events are representational, though unconscious. This contrast provides us one more empirical boundary that any adequate theory of consciousness must explain.

Unaccessed Interpretations of Ambiguous Stimuli

What happens to the "unaccessed" interpretation of an ambiguous visual figure like a Necker Cube when it is not conscious? Does it disappear? Or is it still represented in some sense in the nervous system? In a classic two-channel selective listening experiment, Donald G. MacKay showed in 1973 that an ambiguous word such as "bank" in the sentence "They walked to the bank" could be influenced by unconscious words bearing on one meaning of the ambiguity. Subjects "shadowed" one ear with the conscious sentence while words such as "river" or "money" were presented to the unconscious ear, simultaneous with "bank." When the subjects were given the unconscious word "money," the probability of *bank* being interpreted as a financial institution increased significantly, and vice versa.

In related research, MacKay showed in 1966 that preconscious processing of ambiguous words and phrases slows down when two alternative interpretations are balanced in likelihood, and the ambiguity becomes harder to resolve. This kind of result also indicates that the brain is doing something different in response to unconscious ambiguity. Comparable results were obtained by myself, Jonathan Cohen, Gordon Bower, and Jack Berry, who demonstrated that subjects who were hypnotically primed to feel anger were more likely to pick words with an unconscious angry meaning. Given incomplete sentences such as "At the end of the day, I still had customers to———," angry subjects more often unconsciously chose to fill in the blank with the rather violent "finish off", rather than to more peaceful choices like "help," "attend to," or "handle."

In the case of binocular rivalry, two streams of information are presented to a person's two eyes. Nikos Logothetis and collaborators have found clear electrophysiological evidence that the unaccessed interpretation continues to be processed

David Swinney and others have shown other distinctive aspects of ambiguity-resolution in language perception. A typical experiment in this literature has subjects listen to a sentence fragment ending in an ambiguous word, such as "They all rose." "Rose" can be either a verb or a noun, but in this sentence frame it must be a verb. How long will it take for this syntactic fact to influence sentence processing? To test this, a verb-related word such as "stood" or a noun-related one such as "flower" is presented immediately after "rose." The subject's task is to decide whether this word is a real word or not. If the knowledge about the syntactic category of "rose" is available immediately, it should facilitate response time to "stood;" otherwise, there should be no difference in lexical decision time. A number of investigators have found that for several hundred milliseconds, there is no context effect at all, though the standard priming effect occurs after that. The dead period suggests that there may be a context free automatism that takes over for as long as a few hundred milliseconds after "rose" is presented. This surprising result takes for granted, of course, that there is rapid, sophisticated unconscious processing going on of both the accessed and the nonaccessed meaning.

Contextual Constraints on Perception

Perceptual experiences are constrained by numerous factors that are not themselves conscious. Perhaps the most famous demonstrations of such unconscious constraints were devised by Adelbert Ames in the 1950s, who noted, for example, that the rectangular walls, floor, and ceiling of a normal "carpentered" room actually project trapezoids, not rectangles, onto the retina. Any single retinal projection can be interpreted as the result of an infinite set of trapezoids placed at different angles to the eye. But in Western culture we are exposed mostly to rectangular walls, floors, and ceilings, and we interpret any consistent set of joined trapezoids to be box-shaped with rectangular sides. Hence the "Ames distorted room," which actually consists of joined trapezoidal surfaces, but is perceived as an ordinary rectangular room. Because we assess height in a carpentered environment by implicit comparison to the presumably constant height of the walls, people in an Ames room will appear to grow and shrink dramatically as they walk from one end of the trapezoidal wall to the other. In this way is our conscious experience of size dramatically shaped by unconscious "presuppositions" about the space in which we live. Numerous other examples can be cited. Contextual constraints on perception and comprehension are the rule, not the exception.

Expectations of Specific Stimuli

Expectations about the stimulus world are clearly representations of some sort. For instance, we can immediately detect a violation of an expectation, in any dimension of the expected event. Yet we are not conscious of our expectations regarding the next word in this sentence, though those expectations clearly exist: try substituting a "glorb " in a sentence, for example. Thus, we can apply the Sokolov argument here as well—if the nervous system can detect a change in any dimension of some event, it has a representation of all the mismatchable parameters. Unlike percepts and images, expectations are not objectlike representations—they do not have figure-ground properties, qualitative perceptual dimensions, or a discrete moment of onset and offset in the flow of events.

Stimulus expectations behave in other ways like percepts and images: They are representational, they represent the environment, they sometimes involve ambiguities, they are internally consistent, yet they are not objects of conscious experience. This point is rarely made, but it seems indisputable and theoretically significant.

Images and Inner Speech

Consider now another example of contrastive analysis: the comparison of conscious images with comparable unconscious representations. "Images" are broadly defined to include quasi-perceptual events that occur in the absence of external stimulation in any sensory modality, including inner speech and emotional feelings.

The Conscious Side of Imagery

We are conscious of more than external events. We can reexperience today's breakfast, important events from the past, and hear our own inner speech. People sometimes experience hallucinations, and we all have dreams. Over the past few decades a large and reliable research literature has emerged, especially in the area of visual imagery, so that now a great deal is known about this phenomenon. Imagery in other sense modalities, inner speech, and feelings associated with emotion have seen much less research, but it is hard to see any principled reason why one could not investigate these domains with the same kind of reliability. Images are conscious representations, experienced in the absence of the imagined object. In this book we use the word "imagery" very broadly, to mean all of those quasi-perceptual conscious experiences we can have in the absence of an external stimulus. Visual images resemble visual percepts in a number of respects, and in fact many of the same means of assessment can be used for both perception and imagery—notably, we can use verbal report, which is in practice our primary means for deciding whether people are conscious of something. We can hope that the kind of reliable evidence that has been found in the past few decades regarding visual images can be extended to the study of imagery in the broad sense we are using here, including inner speech and emotional feelings.

Clearly any adequate theory of conscious experience should be able to explain why images are conscious, while the following "stimulus-representations in the absence of the stimulus" are not.

The Unconscious Side of Mental Imagery

Memory Images Before Retrieval

Where is our mental image of yesterday's breakfast before we bring it to mind? If it is accurate, it must in some sense be represented in long-term memory. And after such images are lost from consciousness, some representation must continue to exist, since we can retrieve it again, the first retrieval primes the second one, and so on.

Currently Unrehearsed Items in Working Memory

Comparatively little work has been done on "inner speech" but the vast literature on Working Memory bears on this topic rather closely. In a typical Working Memory experiment, subjects are given a string of unrelated words, letters, or numbers, and requested to retrieve them shortly afterward. A great deal is known of the resulting memory patterns, but relatively little attention has been given to the fact that during the retention interval, only the currently rehearsed item is conscious at any single moment. Thus, Working Memory is closely associated with conscious experience, though not identical to it.

Automatic Mental Images

One of the most intriguing ideas about mental images is that they may fade from consciousness and yet continue to function. Hard evidence to that effect has been developed by John Pani among others.

Contrasts Involving Attention

This class of events also overlaps with previous categories, but it emphasizes the selective and directive aspects. That is, there is always perceptual information that might be quite conscious, but which is excluded from consciousness because of a competing stream of input. Further, we make the traditional distinction between voluntary attention, which is itself preceded by a conscious decision to pay attention to something, and involuntary attention, in which an unexpected stimulus disrupts the attended stream.

Attended versus Unattended Messages

There is obviously a difference in consciousness of an attended and an unattended stream of information. However, aspects of the unattended stream frequently can become conscious. In the standard "shadowing" paradigm where subjects repeat a continuous stream of speech in one ear while another one is presented to the other ear, subjects can typically identify voice quality in the "unattended" channel, though single words have been repeated as much as thirty-five times without subjects being able to report them, according to Donald Norman.

Interruption of, and Influence on, the Attended Stream

A loud noise in the unattended channel can interrupt clearly conscious information in the attended channel. Further, "significant" stimuli in the unattended channel (such as one's name) can disrupt the conscious stream, even when they are not particularly loud. This can be contrasted with events in the unattended channel that change the interpretation of the conscious stream of information, but without disrupting it overtly. (see above) Thus unconscious events can influence the interpretation of simultaneous conscious events.

Voluntary versus Involuntary Attention

We can ask someone to pay attention to something in the unattended channel voluntarily. In this case, conscious information (our request) precedes the shift in attention. Alternatively we can make someone pay attention to something in the unattended channel by presenting a loud noise, the name of the subject, and perhaps a variety of other "significant" stimuli that will disrupt the conscious stream of information without voluntary involvement by the subject. In that sense, events preceding voluntary attention are conscious, while those preceding involuntary attention are not.

Dishabituation of Orienting

On the basis of research with the Orienting Response (OR), we know that a change in any parameter of any habituated stimulus may elicit a new OR. Since the OR is clearly associated with consciousness (at least in humans), we can claim that, while predictable repetitions in stimulation remain unconscious, changes in this predictable pattern tend to become conscious.

Thinking: Spontaneous Problem-Solving

Most Thinking Is Inexplicit

Entirely conscious problem-solving, such as working out an arithmetic problem on paper, is quite rare. Rather, we tend to solve problems "spontaneously": to be conscious of the stage of problem assignment, not conscious of some intermediate stage, and conscious again of the solution of the problem.

These are the famous phenomena of problem incubation and the "Aha!" experience, frst discussed by Gestalt psychologists like Köhler in the 1920s. One is conscious of the stage of problem definition, but not of the incubation stage, in which the problem is presumably moving toward solution. Finally, the problem "comes to mind" again, and the solution is clear. George Miller and others have pointed out that we are typically conscious of the *results* of mental processes but not of the mental processes themselves. But very significantly, we are also conscious of the stage of problem definition. Further, in a reasonably complex problem we are usually conscious of intermediate steps on the road to a solution.

Word Retrieval and Question Answering

We may be conscious of an incomplete sentence, unconscious of the retrieval process, and conscious again of the arrival of the proper word. Similarly, if someone asks a question, we are conscious of the question, usually not of the process of searching for an answer, and conscious again of the arrival of the answer. While the time intervals involved in these commonplace processes are much shorter than in the case of creative mathematical problem-solving, the overall pattern seems the same.

Recall from Long-Term Memory

The same may be said of other recall processes. We can retrieve the image of the American flag, but the process whereby we do so is utterly opaque. Free association and numerous other memory tasks have the same character.

Action Planning and Control

We may have some conscious planning process about the next sentence we intend to say (though not all of an intention is conscious, as James pointed out), and we have no access to the process whereby our conscious plans are converted into detailed movements; however, we can typically monitor conscious perceptual feedback from the results of an action.

Perceptual Reorganization

We can see two interpretations of a Necker Cube, but we have little conscious insight into the process that brings us from one to the other. We may be solving a visual puzzle or trying to understand a sentence spoken in a very heavy dialect; in either case, we are conscious of some early information, often appearing to be very complex and difficult to organize, but this early organization is succeeded by a second, simpler conscious experience without any awareness of the details of intermediate processes.

Thus, the conscious-unconscious-conscious pattern of problem solving processes is very general indeed. It can be found in explicit, deliberate problem-solving in mathematics; in minor everyday problem-solving, such as question answering; in memory recall; in action planning and execution; and in perceptual organization. Especially in the last case, it is clear that the problem-solving process does not need to be intentional in the usual sense. All we need to do is be aware of the Necker Cube, and suddenly we may see it become reorganized.

One intriguing possibility in this regard is that James's "stream of consciousness," which appears as a series of "flights and perches" of the mind on different topics, could actually consist of an interwoven series of such conscious-unconscious-conscious triads. It may be that we are continuously engaged in a number of overlapping problem-solving processes, in which unconscious mechanisms attempt to resolve issues posed consciously, returning their answers to consciousness as well. These answers may, in turn, provide the conscious input for another unconscious problem-solving process.

Consciousness and Some Learning Phenomena

Developing Automaticity with Practice in Predictable Tasks

It is commonly observed that when we begin learning a difficult skill, we may be conscious of many details; after skill acquisition we are conscious of much less; and if the skill is disrupted in some way, we become conscious of some missing ingredient. Indeed, Ellen Langer and Nancy Imber have shown that subjects learning a simple coding task cannot retrieve the number of steps in the task once it has become automatic, although this is quite easy before automatization of the task. This pattern suggests that conscious involvement may help to integrate

new information, but that it is not required for the smooth, routine execution of complex tasks. (There is obviously a close relationship
between this pattern and the habituation phenomena discussed in the
table at the end of this appendix). When automatic execution of a
skilled task is disrupted, as in reading upside-down, the opposite
occurs: we tend to become more conscious of the details of the task
(Baars, 1988).

Loss of Conscious Access to Visual Information that Nonetheless Continues to Inform Problem-Solving

A particularly interesting case of this pattern exists in skilled use of
imagery. Lynn Cooper and Roger Shepard already noted that subjects
who are skilled in their classic mental rotation task often report losing
awareness of their own processes. Nevertheless, the unconscious
"image" continues to rotate at the same rate, as shown by reaction
time, matching to sample, and the like. Similarly, John Pani has shown
that mental images required to solve a problem become less consciously available with practice but can reemerge when the subject encounters unexpected difficulty.

Implicit Learning of Miniature Grammars

Subjects who are given a set of stimuli generated by a simple "grammar" unconsciously induce the underlying grammar as shown by successful recognition of novel cases generated by the same rule systems.
Because humans routinely learn numerous rule systems without being
able ever to state the rules, this finding has implications for a great deal
of actual learning. It is one among many indications that consciousness "focuses" many unconscious capabilities upon problems to be
solved in the world.

Capability Contrasts

Whatever we do really well, we tend to do unconsciously, from speaking
to seeing to playing piano. This observation has led some psychologists to
wonder why consciousness is needed at all. To get at this question of the
role of consciousness, we can conduct another contrastive analysis,
focused on the capabilities of comparable conscious and unconscious
processes. The table at the end of this appendix presents a basic set of
such Capability Contrasts. Notice that purely conscious processes are

handicapped by low computational efficiency: they are rather inefficient (slow, prone to error, and vulnerable to interference), serial, and limited in capacity. Consider mentally multiplying 23 × 79. For most of us this is not very easy to do, and the more the steps are conscious, the more difficult it is. Yet mental multiplication is trivial in complexity compared to the vast amount of processing that is needed to analyze the syntax of this sentence. But syntactic analysis is of course entirely unconscious. Mental arithmetic can become more efficient with practice by letting highly predictable steps become automatic and unconscious, but that illustrates the same point, that efficiency in computational processes is achieved when some algorithm becomes unconscious.

Purely conscious mental manipulations have a high rate of errors, are slow, and interfere with each other, suggesting that performing efficient symbolic computation is not the primary function of consciousness.

But the computational drawbacks of experience are balanced by clear advantages: Consciousness has a *vast range* of possible contents, it enables novel *access* to an astonishing number of skills and knowledge sources, and it shows exquisite context-sensitivity.

As an example of its vast range, consider all the possible percepts, images, memories, concepts, intentions, fringe experiences, and the like of which we can be conscious. As one poetic student put it, we can be conscious of everything from the "rumbling of our stomach to the return of a theme in a Bach cantata."

A conscious event, like this sentence, can access new information in memory, combine knowledge from different sources in the brain in novel ways, and trigger unconscious rule systems that will pick up errors in any level of analysis—in the meaning, syntax, word level, sound, intonation, or printing of this "snetnecne."

The context sensitivity of consciousness can easily be shown to permeate whole domains, such as perception, thinking, or language. Take the predominance of lexical ambiguity, the fact that most words in natural languages have multiple meanings. The *Oxford English Dictionary*, for example, devotes seventy-five thousand words to the many different meanings of the little word "set." Thus, whatever we experience is shaped by unconscious processes, just like a theater in which we see only the actors onstage, but not all the people behind the scenes who make it all work. If the same actors were off stage (unconscious) their actions would not be contextualized by the entire supportive apparatus of the theater. The context sensitivity of conscious events extends far beyond language to perception, action control, memory, problem solving, et cetera. But there is no evidence that novel combinations of subliminal words can be understood unconsciously. Likewise, when we make a navigational error simply because we are so used to turning right on the street going home, the less conscious we are, the more we are likely to make the error. The less conscious some event is, the less it is sensitive to context.

Unconscious processes have their own advantages, however. Unconscious automatisms, such as the ones that control nearly all aspects of the act of reading, show impressive speed and accuracy in routine matters, a tendency to perform parallel or concurrent processing whenever possible, and, when all unconscious resources are taken together, a vast capacity. But of course there is constant interaction between conscious and unconscious processes. In listening to a friend describe last night's party, we follow the conscious flow of sound, words, and meaning with no awareness of the complex acoustic, phonological, morphological, lexical, syntactic, semantic, intonational, and pragmatic processes happening at the same time, all of which are needed for us to become aware of the message.

Yet we can easily prove that these sophisticated unconscious processes are going on all the time. Should our friend commit any error, such as saying "entomology" instead of "etymology," we would immediately detect the error (if we were paying attention), even though it occurred at any of a dozen different levels of analysis. Further, concurrent with all this fast, complex, and unconscious linguistic activity, we also maintain balance and upright posture, represent predictable aspects of all incoming stimuli, and shape our actions in terms of the social and pragmatic demands of the situation.

In the laboratory, the limitations of purely unconscious language processing have been highlighted in selective attention studies. If we receive two dense flows of information, such as two simultaneous stories, one in each ear, or two different ball games shown on the same television set, we can follow only a single, consistent flow of the action. Under these conditions we can present information to the "unattended channel," the ear one is not listening to, for example. In general, it has been found that semantic priming from individual words in the unattended channel can influence the experience of the conscious, attended channel. Thus, the word "money" in the unattended message can bias understanding of the word "bank" toward "financial institution" instead of "shoreline of a river". However, the information in the unconscious channel does not extend to the meaning of longer passages.

Consistent patterns of evidence now begin to emerge from the contrastive analysis. We see the interplay of a serial, integrated, and very limited stream of consciousness with an unconscious system that is distributed, composed of autonomous modules, and of enormous collective capacity.

Here is a summary table of the distinctive capabilities of both conscious and unconscious mental processes. The details are explained in this appendix, and in previous chapters. Here is your data. Can you design a theory that fits? Good luck!

Table 1
Capabilities of Conscious and Unconscious Processes

Conscious Processes	_Unconscious Processes_
1. Computationally inefficient: e.g., mental arithmetic.	1. Very efficient in routine tasks: e.g., syntax.
Many errors, relatively low speed, and mutual interference between conscious processes.	Few errors, high speed, and little mutual interference.
2. Great range of contents.	2. Each routine process has a limited range of contents.
Great ability to relate different conscious contents to each other.	Each routine process is relatively isolated and autonomous.
Great ability to relate conscious events to their unconscious contexts.	Each routine process is relatively contextfree
3. High internal consistency at any single moment, seriality over time, and limited processing capacity.	3. Routine, unconscious processes are diverse, can sometimes operate in parallel, and together have great processing capacity.
4. The clearest conscious contents are perceptual or quasi-perceptual (e.g. imagery, skill learning, problem-solving, action control, etc.).	4. Unconscious processes are involved in _all_ mental tasks, from perception and imagery, inner speech, and internally into memory, knowledge representation and access, generated bodily feelings, etc.).

Selected References

Anderson, John R. (1983) *The architecture of cognition*. Cambridge, MA: Harvard University Press.

Baars, Bernard J. (1986) *The cognitive revolution in psychology*. New York: Guilford Press

Baars, Bernard J. (1988) *A cognitive theory of consciousness*. Cambridge: Cambridge University Press.

Baars, Bernard J. (Ed.) (1992) *The experimental psychology of human error: Exploring the architecture of voluntary control*. New York: Plenum Press, Cognition and Language Series.

Baars, Bernard J. (1993) How does a serial, integrated and very limited stream of consciousness emerge from a nervous system that is mostly unconscious, distributed, and of enormous capacity? In G. Bock and J. Marsh (Eds.), *CIBA Symposium on Experimental and Theoretical Studies of Consciousness* (pp. 282–290). London: John Wiley and Sons.

Baars, Bernard J. (1994) Why volition is a foundation issue for psychology. *Consciousness & Cognition*, 2, 281–309.

Baars, Bernard J. (1996a) *Sensory projection areas of the cortex may provide a conscious global workspace for a massively distributed unconscious brain*. Second International Conference on Consciousness, University of Arizona, Tucson, AZ.

Baars, Bernard J. (1996b) A thoroughly empirical approach to consciousness. In N. Block, O. Flanagan, and G. Guzeldere (Eds.) *Consciousness in phi-*

losophy and science. Cambridge, MA: MIT Press/Bradford Books.

Baars, Bernard J. (in press) Psychology in a world of sentient, self-knowing beings: A modest utopian fantasy. In R. L. Solso (Ed.) *The science of the mind: The 21st century*. Cambridge, MA: MIT Press.

Baars, Bernard J. (in press) Quantum quibbles: The evidence that any theory of conscious experience must explain. In P. Pylkkanen & P. Pylkko (Eds.) *New directions in cognitive science: The lapland symposium*.

Baars, Bernard J., Cohen, Jonathan, Bower, Gordon H., and Berry, Jack (1992) Some caveats on testing the Freudian Slip Hypothesis: Problems in systematic replication. In Bernard J. Baars (Ed.), *Experimental slips and human error: Exploring the architecture of cognition*. New York: Plenum Press.

Baars, Bernard J. & McGovern, K. A. (1994) Consciousness. In V. Ramachandran (Ed.), *Encyclopedia of behavior*, New York: Academic Press.

Baars, Bernard J. Fehling, M., McGovern, K., & LaPolla, M. (1996). Competition for a conscious global workspace leads to coherent, flexible action. In J. Cohen & J. Schooler (Eds.), *Scientific approaches to consciousness: The 25th Carnegie Symposium in Cognition* Hillsdale, NJ: Erlbaum.

Baars, Bernard J. & Newman, J. (1994). A neurobiological interpretation of Global Workspace Theory. In A. Revonsuo & M. Camppinen (Eds.), *Consciousness in philosopy and cognitive neuroscience* Hillsdale NJ: Erlbaum.

Barfield, Owen (1953/1988) *History in English words*. Great Barrington, MA: Lindisfarne Press.

Bisiach, Eduardo, and Geminiani, Guliano (1991) Anosognosia related to hemiplegia and hemianopia. In George P. Prigatano and Daniel L. Schacter (Eds.), *Awareness of deficit after brain injury: Clinical and theoretical issues*. New York: Oxford University Press.

Bogen, Joseph E. (1995) On the neurophysiology of consciousness: I. An overview. *Consciousness & Cognition, 4,* 15–24.

Bransford, John D. (1979) *Human cognition*. Belmont, CA: Wadsworth.

Calvin, W. H., and Ojemann, G. A. (1994) *Conversations with Neil's brain: The neural nature of thought and language*. New York: Addison-Wesley.

Carlson, Neil R. (1991) *Physiology of behavior*. 4th Edition. Boston, MA: Allyn & Bacon.

Cooper, L. A., and Shepard, R. N. (1973) *Chronometric studies of the rotation of mental images*. In W. G. Chase (Ed.), Visual information processing. New York: Academic Press.

Crick, Francis (1984) The function of the thalamic reticular complex: The searchlight hypothesis. *Proceedings of the National Academy of Sciences, USA 81,* 4586–4590.

Crick, Francis (1993) *The astonishing hypothesis: The scientific search for the soul,* New York: Scribner's.

Crick, Francis, and Koch, Christof (1990) Towards a neurobiological theory of consciousness. *Seminars in Neuroscience, 2,* 263–275.

Dallenbach, K. M. (1951) A puzzle-picture with a new principle of conceal-
ment. *American Journal of Psychology, 64*, 431-433.

Darwin, Charles (c. 1838) *Old and useless notes.* In P. H. Barrett and H. Gru-
ber, *Darwin on man: A psychological study of scientific creativity.* London:
Wildwood House, 1974.

Dennett, Daniel C. (1978) Toward a cognitive theory of consciousness. In D. C.
Dennett (Ed.), *Brainstorms.* Cambridge, MA: Bradford Books/MIT Press.

Dennett, Daniel C. (1991) *Consciousness explained.* New York: Little, Brown.

Dennett, Daniel C., and Kinsbourne, Marcel (1992) Time and the observer:
The where and when of consciousness in the brain. *Brain and Behavioral Sciences, 15*, 183–247.

Descartes, René (1637) *Fourth set of replies, II, Sixth Meditation, Philosophical
Writings of Descartes.* Tr. J. Cottingham, R. Stoothoff, and D. Murdoch.
London: Cambridge University Press.

Edelman, Gerald M. (1989) *The remembered present: A biological theory of
consciousness.* New York: Basic Books.

Einstein, Albert (1949) *Autobiographical Notes.* In P. A. Shilpp (Ed.), *Albert
Einstein—Philosopher—Scientist* (Vol. 1) New York: Harper & Row.

Ellenberger, Henri F. (1970) *The discovery of the unconscious: The history and
evolution of dynamic psychiatry.* New York: Basic Books.

Erdelyi, Matthew (1985) *Psychoanalysis: Freud's cognitive psychology.* San Fran-
cisco: Freeman.

Flanagan, Owen (1992) *Consciousness reconsidered.* Cambridge, MA: MIT
Press.

Fraisse, P. (1963) *The psychology of time.* New York: Harper & Row.

Freud, Anna (1946) *The ego and the mechanisms of defense.* New York: International Universities Press.

Gazzaniga, Michael S. (1995) Consciousness and the cerebral hemispheres.
In M. S. Gazzaniga, (Ed.), *The cognitive neurosciences.* Cambridge, MA:
Bradford Books / MIT Press.

Ghiselin, Brewster (1952) *The Creative Process.* New York: Mentor.

Gibbs,Raymond W., Jr., (1994) *The poetics of mind: Figurative thought, language, and understanding.* Cambridge: Cambridge University Press.

Gregory, Richard (1966) *Eye and brain.* New York: McGraw-Hill.

Hadamard, Jacques (1945) *The psychology of invention in the mathematical field.*
Princeton, NJ: Princeton University Press.

Haier, R. J., B. V. Siegel, Jr., A. MacLachlan, E. Soderberg, S. Lotternberg, and
M. S. Buchsbaum (1992) Regional glucose metabolic changes after
learning complex visuospatial/motor task. *Brain Research, 570*, 134–143.

Hilgard, Ernest R. (1977) *Divided consciousness: Multiple controls in human
thought and action.* New York: Wiley.

Hobson, J. Allan (1989) *The dreaming brain.* NY: Basic Books.

James, William (1890) *The principles of psychology.* Cambridge, MA: Harvard
University Press, 1983.

James, William (1893) *Psychology: The briefer course*. New York: Harper and Row.

Kinney, H. C. , Korein, J., Panigrahy, A., Dikkes, P., and Goode, R. (1994) Neuropathological findings in the brain of Karen Ann Quinlan: The role of the thalamus in the persistent vegetative state. *New England Journal of Medicine, 330*, 1469–1475.

Kohler, Wolfgang (1929) *Gestalt psychology*. New York: Liveright.

Kosslyn, Stephen M. (1980) *Image and mind*. Cambridge, MA: Harvard University Press.

Kosslyn, Stephen M. (1988) Aspects of a cognitive neuroscience of mental imagery. *Science, 240*, 1621–1626.

LaBerge, Stephen (1985) *Lucid dreaming*. New York: Ballantine

LaBerge, Stephen and Kahan, Tracey (1994) Lucid dreaming as metacognition: Implications for cognitive science. *Consciousness and Cognition, 3*, 246–264.

Lakoff, George (1987) *Women, fire, and other dangerous things: What categories reveal about the mind*. Chicago: University of Chicago Press.

Lakoff, George, and Johnson, Mark (1980) *Metaphors we live by*. Chicago: University of Chicago Press.

Langer, Ellen J., and Imber, L. G. (1979) When practice makes imperfect: Debilitating effects of overlearning. *Journal of Personality and Social Psychology, 37*, 2014–2024.

Levelt, W. J. M. (1989) *Speaking: From intention to articulation*. Cambridge, MA: MIT Press.

Lindsay, Peter, and Norman, Donald A. (1977) *Human information processing*. New York: Academic Press.

Llinás, Rodolfo, and Ribary, U. (1992) Rostrocaudal scan in human brain: A global characteristic of the 40-Hz response during sensory input. In E. Basar and T. Bullock (Eds.), *Induced rhythms in the brain* (pp. 147–154). Boston: Birkhäuser.

Logothetis, Nikos K., and Schall, Jeffrey D. (1989) Neuronal correlates of subjective visual perception. *Science, 245*, 761–763.

MacKay, Donald G. (1973) Aspects of a theory of comprehension, memory, and attention. *Quarterly Journal of Experimental Psychology, 25*, 22–40.

McNeill, David (1966) Developmental psycholinguistics. In F. Smith and G.A. Miller (Eds.), *The genesis of language: A psycholinguistic approach*. Cambridge, MA: MIT Press.

Mangan, Bruce (1993) Taking phenomenology seriously: The "fringe" and its implications for cognitive research. *Consciousness and Cognition, 2*, 89–108.

Marcel, Anthony J., and Bisiach, Eduardo (Eds.) (1988) *Consciousness in contemporary science*. Oxford: Clarendon Press.

Milne, R. W. (1982) Predicting garden-path sentences. *Cognitive Science, 6*, 349–374.

Newell, Alan (1990) *Unified theories of cognition.* Cambridge, MA: Harvard University Press.

Newell, Alan and Simon, Herbert A. (1972) *Human problem solving.* Englewood Cliffs, NJ: Prentice Hall.

Newman, J. and Baars, B. J. (1993) A neural attentional model for access to consciousness: A global workspace perspective. *Concepts in Neuroscience* 4 (2), 255–290.

Pani, John (1982) *A functionalist approach to mental imagery.* Twenty-third Meeting of the Society for Psychonomic Science, Baltimore.

Paulescu, E., Frith, D., Frackowiak, R. S. J. (1993) The neural correlates of the verbal component of working memory, *Nature, 362,* 342–345.

Pinker, Steven (1994) *The language instinct: How the mind creates language.* New York: HarperPerennial.

Plato, *The Republic. Great Dialogues of Plato.* Tr. W. H. D. Rouse (1956) New York: Mentor Books.

Polanyi, Michael (1966) *The tacit dimension.* Garden City, NY: Doubleday.

Posner, Michael I., and Raichle, Marcus E. (1994) *Images of mind.* New York: Scientific American Library.

Reason, James (1984) Lapses of attention in everyday life. In R. Parasuraman and D. R. Davies (Eds.), *Varieties of attention.* New York: Academic Press.

Reber, Arthur (1993) *Implicit learning.* New York: Oxford University Press.

Rock, Irving (1984) *Perception.* New York: W.H. Freeman.

Rosch, Eleanor, and Lloyd, B. (1978) *Cognition and categorization.* Lawrence, NJ: Erlbaum.

Ryle, Gilbert (1949) *The concept of mind.* London: Hutchinson.

Searle, John R. (1994) *The rediscovery of the mind.* Cambridge, MA: Bradford Books/MIT Press.

Sokolov, E .N. (1963) *Perception and the conditioned reflex.* New York: Macmillan.

Sperry, Roger W. (1966), Brain bisection and mechanisms of consciousness. In John C. Eccles (Ed.), *Brain and conscious experience.* New York: Springer-Verlag.

Spitzer, R. L. (Ed.) (1979) *Diagnostic and statistical manual of mental disorders.* (DSM-III). Washington, D.C.: American Psychiatric Association.

Wegner, Daniel (1989) *White bears and other unwanted thoughts.* New York: Viking.

Weiskrantz, Larry (1986) *Blindsight: A case study and its implications.* Oxford: Clarendon.

Winson, Jonathan (1985) *Brain and psyche: The biology of the unconscious.* New York: Doubleday.

Zeki, Semir (1993) *A vision of the brain.* London: Blackwell Scientific.

The author gratefully acknowledges permission to reprint the following:

Insert 1 is reprinted from *Brain Research, 570,* by Richard J. Haier et al, "Regional Glucose Metabolic Changes after Learning a Complex Visuospatial/Motor task: A Positron Emission tomographic Study," 134-143, copyright © 1992 with kind permission from Elsevier Science-NL, Sara Burgerhartstraat 25, 1053 KV Amsterdam, The Netherlands.

Inserts 2 and 3, and Figures 3-2, and 4-1 are from or adapted from *Images of Mind* by Posner and Raichle. Copyright © 1994 by Scientific American Library. Used with permission of W. H. Freeman and Company.

Insert 4 is reprinted with permission from *Nature,* by E. Paulesu, et. al, "The Neural correlates of the Verbal Component of Working Memory." Copyright © 1993, Macmillan Magazines Ltd.

The various William James quotes throughout are from *The Principles of Psychology* by William James. Copyright © 1981 by the President and Fellows of Harvard College. Reprinted by permission of Harvard University Press.

Selected text excerpts and Figures 2-2, 2-3, 3-4, 5-2, 6-1, 7-1, 7-2, and Table 1 are from Bernard J. Baars, *A Cognitive Theory of Consciousness.* Copyright © 1988, and are reprinted with the permission of Cambridge University Press.

Figure 3-1 is from Semir Zeki, *A Vision of the Brain,* copyright © 1993 by Blackwell Scientific.

Figure 4-2 is from Tracey L. Kahan & Stephen LaBerge, Lucid Dreaming as Metacognition: Implications for Cognitive Science, copyright © by Academic Press.

Figure 5-1 is from *American Journal of Psychology 64:* 431-33. Copyright 1951 by the Board of Trustees of the University of Illinois. Used with permission of the University of Illinois Press.

Figure 5-3 is from W. H. Calvin/G. Ojeman, *Conversations with Neil's Brain* (from page 182), © 1994 by William H. Calvin and George Ojemann. Reprinted by permission of Addison-Wesley Longman Inc.

Index

absorption. *See also* suggestibility,
102–108
access function of consciousness,
163–164
access of self to consciousness, 153,
161
access, consciousness creates 6–7,
163–164, 179
action control, 64, 177
ambiguity, in words, 26–27, 118–122,
170–173, 180
Ames, Adelbert, 173
amnesia, 151
Anderson, John R., 36
animal consciousness, 31–33
anosognosia, 148–149
Area V1 as a coordinating map, 71
Aristotle, 31, 36, 74,
artists break up conventionalized experience, 91
ASSC (Association for the Scientific
Study of Consciousness), xii
attention vs. consciousness, 98–101
attention, as a selective capacity, 29,

95–101, 175–177
attention, spotlight of, 5
attentional network, 100
auditory consciousness, Fig. 3–3
automaticity of practiced skills, 17, 29,
134–137, 139–141, 175, 178–179
automatisms, wanted and unwanted,
139–141
Autonomic Nervous System, 132

Baddeley, Alan, xi
Barlow, Owen, 82–83
behaviorism, xii, 16, 23, 131, 166–167
Békésy, Georg, 89
beliefs, unconscious, 128–129
Berkeley, George, 77–78
binding, spatial, 71
binding, temporal, 71
binocular fusion, 88–89
binocular rivalry, 172
biofeedback, 58–59, 133, 138–139, 141
Bisiach, Eduardo, 128, 148–149
blindsight, 66–69, 71
Block, Ned, 34

Bogen, Joseph, x, 30
brain imaging, 29, 71, 74, 88
breakthroughs to consciousness, 27
Broadbent, Donald E. 22–23

capabilities of conscious vs. uncon-
    scious processes, 179–182
Cardeña, Etzel, 161
Carroll, Lewis, 90
Cartesian Theater Fallacy, xi, 5
Chevreul pendulum, 137
cognitive neuroscience, xii
cognitive psychology, xii
cognitive revolution in psychology, xii
cognitive science, xii
coherence of conscious contents, 87–90
coma. See wakefulness and coma
conceptual context, 128–129
concreteness of images, 77–78
conscious construction of reality,
    105–111
conscious control of action, 130–141
context system in the brain, 126–128,
context, xii, 115–129
contextualizing function of conscious-
    ness, 163
contrastive phenomenology (contrastive
    analysis), 12, 18–22, 29, 30, 34, 182
Cooper, Lynn, 179
cortex, frontal, 32, 64
cortex, posterior (sensory), 32–33,
cortex, visual consciousness in, 64–72,
    100
cortex, visual, "what" and "where" path-
    ways, 71
Crick, Francis, x, xi, 5–6, 35, 36, 71

Dallenbach Cow, 117
Darwin, Charles, xii, 15, 34, 167
decision–making and executive function
    of consciousness, 159
decontextualization, 126
Dell, Gary, 76,
Dement, William, 110
Dennett, Daniel C., x, 35, 143, 145,
    161
depersonalization, 126, 149–150
derealization, 150

Descartes, René, 15, 31, 81
dissociative disorders, 152
distributed (decentralized) style of func-
    tioning, 6
dreaming, 95, 105–111

Edelman, Gerald, x, 31, 35, 69–70
EEG (electroencephalography), 14, 29,
    33, 109,110
Einstein, Albert, 85–86, 128–129
Ekman, Paul, 132
error–detection and editing functions of
    consciousness, 160
executive functions (self as agent), 100
expectations and intentions, 122–125,
    144, 173–174
eye movements, 146–147

facial anastomosis, 132
facial expressions of emotion, voluntary
    vs. spontaneous, 132
Farah, Martha, 74
federal style of functioning, 140–141
feedback, conscious (biofeedback),
    138–139
Feyman diagrams, 83
fixedness of context, 118, 119–122
Flanagan, Owen, 35
flexibility function of consciousness,
    159–160
forty-Hertz hypothesis, 31, 72
fovea (foveal fixations), 39–40, 106
Freud, Sigmund, 16, 84–85, 107, 111
fringe (vague) consciousness, xiii,
    43–44, 86, 180
fugue (amnesic flight), 126, 150–151
functions of consciousness, 157–164,
    166

Gazzaniga, Michael, x–xi, 147–148
Gemiani, Giulio, 147–148
Gestalt psychology, 92
Gibbs, Raymon, 82
Global Workspace model, x–xi
global broadcasting (distribution) of
    information, 7, 52
global coordination and control, 7
goals, dominant (see intentions), 137

habit intrusion as a source of catastrophic error, 134–135
habituated (postperceptual) representation, 170–171
Haier, Richard, 29
Helmholtz, Herrmann von, 146–147
hemispherectomy, 30
Hilgard, Ernest R., 152
Hobson, J. Allan, 107
homunculus fallacy, 143–145
homunculus, sensorimotor, 145
Hume, David, 86
Huxley, Thomas Henry, 166
hypnosis. *See* suggestibility

ideas (abstract concepts), 78–94,
   103–105
ideomotor theory, William James',
   104–105, 130–141, 160, 162
imageable "handles" for abstractions,
   80–82
imagery, 33, 62–94, 73–78, 133–138,
   141, 174–175
implicit learning and thinking,
   176–177, 179
inner narrative, 40, 75
inner senses. *See* imagery and inner
   speech
inner speech (self–talk), 63, 75, 88,
   174–175
intentions and expectations. *See also*
   volition, 122–125
internal consistency of conscious contents, 87–90, 95
interruption of the conscious stream,
   106–107, 176
intralaminar nuclei of the thalamus
   (ILN), 29, 71–72
introspectionism, xii

Jabberwocky, 25, 90
James, William, ix, 15–16, 35, 36, 95,
   96, 104–105, 123–126, 130–134,
   136, 137, 140–141, 142, 157, 166
Johnson, Mark, 81–82

Kinsbourne, Marcel, x–xi, 5
Köhler, Wolfgang, 177

Kosslyn, Stephen, xi, 73–74

LaBerge, Stephen, 109–111
Lakoff, George, 21, 81–82
Langer, Ellen, 135–137
learning and adaptation function of
   consciousness, 161–162, 178–179
lexicon, mental, 40, 46, 48, 159, 177
limited capacity of consciousness,
   37–61
Llinás, Rodolfo, x, 31, 71
lucid dreaming, 109–111

MacKay, Donald G., 26–27, 171–172
mammalian brain, 32
Marcel, Anthony, 170
Maslow, Abraham, 143
meaning (semantic coding), 78–79,
   84–88, 90–94
meaning, conscious access to, 78–84
meaning, unconscious, 4
medical student syndrome. *See also* suggestibility, 104
memory, long–term. *See also* working
   memory, 177
metacognition, and skepticism,
   101–103
metaphors, 81–84
mind's eye. *See* imagery,
mind–body problem, xii, 166–167
Minsky, Marvin, xi
Moray, Neville, 25
Mozart, Wolfgang Amadeus, 12, 50–51,
   81
multiple layers of conscious contents,
   91
multiple personality disorder, 126,
   151–153

Necker Cube, 87–88, 171, 178
neglect, parietal damage 126–128
neural nets, xi, 7
neurons, nerve cells, 6, 18–20
Newell, Alan, xi, 36
Newman, James, xi,
Newton, Isaac, 82

orientation to gravity, as context, 116

orienting response, 170–171, 176

Pavlov, I. P., 36
perceptual organization, 178
PET scans, 18–19, 29, 35, 71, 74
    75–77, 100
phobia (visual imagery in), 76–77
phospemes, in visual cortex, 101
Plato, 37, 77, 82–83
Plato's Allegory of the Cave, 5, 36
Posner, Michael I., x, 35, 100
post–traumatic stress disorder, 76, 126
postmodernism, 126
preperceptual processes, 170
primary visual cortex (area V1), 64–73
priming of contexts, 118–119, 125, 170
prioritizing function of consciousness,
    158
problem–solving function of conscious-
    ness, 159
problem–solving, spontaneous, 176–177
prototypes, 79–84
pseudobulbar palsy, 132
Putnam, Frank W., 151

qualia, sensory qualities, 21–22, 34, 74
qualia, unconscious representations of, 22
quality, as an invented concept, 82–83
Quinlan, Karen Ann, 28–31

Ramachandran, V. S., 105
Rapport, Nathan, 110–111
reading, automatic and upside–down,
    20–21
reality, conscious construction of,
    105–106
Reason, James, 134
redundancy effects, 92–93
reentrant loops, 69–70
reports, verifiable public, 4, 23, 34,
    109–110
reptilian brain, 32
reticular formation, 27, 32
Revonsuo, Antti, 205
Rosch, Eleanor, 79–80
Ryle, Gilbert, 143–144

Sacks, Oliver, 149

Schacter, Daniel, xi
schizophrenia, 26, 76–77
Searle, John, 35
self as agent, 143–144
self as narrative interpreter, 147–149
self as observer, 143–144
self as unifying context, xii, 142–153
self-alien syndromes, 146–152
self-as-subject vs. self-as-object, 16
self–other differentiation, 147
semantic satiation, 92–93
sensorimotor self, 146–147
sensory (perceptual) consciousness, 32,
    62–94
sensory (posterior) cortex, 64
sensory bias of consciousness, 62–94,
    76
sensory field, events outside of, 84
Shakespeare, William, 39, 85
Shepard, Roger, 179
signal anxiety, 84–85
similarities between sensations and
    ideas, 86–88
Simon, Herbert A., xi, 36
simultaneous sensory and abstract con-
    sciousness, 90–93
skepticism, and suspension of disbelief,
    103–105
Skinner, B. F., 16, 169
sleep, deep, 108
Sokolov, E. N., 170–171
speech and language, 33
speech, brain areas, 75
Spiegel, David, 152, 161
split-brain patient, 147–148
spotlight of attention, 42–46, 61,
    95–111, 115, 133–134, 145
stream of consciousness, 96, 125–126
stress and dissociative disorders, 152
structure and cohesion of the conscious
    stream, 24
subjective vs. objective evidence, xii, 4,
    33, 166–167
subliminal stimuli, 17, 20–22, 170
suggestibility (hypnotizability), 103–105
surprise (orienting response), 107
suspension of disbelief. See also skepti-
    cism, absorption, 103

Swinney, David, 172

thalamus, 28–32
theater director. *See also* self, 142–153
theater model, theater metaphor, x, 5–7, 113, 157
theater stage, theater audience, 37–61, 45–47, 52–53, 72–73
thinking and metacognition, 101–102
thought avoidance, 84–85
tip-of-the-foot state, 124
tip-of-the-tongue state, 122–125
trauma, as violation of self–system, 146
Tulving, Endel, 107
two-channel experiment, 22–27, 106–107

unconscious mental processes, 16–18

variable, consciousness as, 10–35

vast access created by consciousness, 37–61
Vedanta philosophy, 6, 36
virtual reality computers, 105
visual agnosia, 67, 92
visual consciousness, 71, 74, 115–116
visual field, 73, 126–128
volition, voluntary control, 130–141
voluntary attention, 101–102, 176
voluntary control as conscious control, 131

wakefulness and coma, 27–31, 32, 71–72
waking construction of reality will. *See also* volition, 106
Winson, Jonathan, 107
word boundaries, perceived, 90–91
working memory, 42–48, 57, 75, 78, 100, 103, 159, 163, 175